THE VIETNAM
ANTIWAR MOVEMENT
IN AMERICAN HISTORY

Other titles *in American History*

IN
AMERICAN
HISTORY

THE VIETNAM ANTIWAR MOVEMENT IN AMERICAN HISTORY

Anita Louise McCormick

Enslow Publishers, Inc.

40 Industrial Road	PO Box 38
Box 398	Aldershot
Berkeley Heights, NJ 07922	Hants GU12 6BP
USA	UK

http://www.enslow.com

Library of Congress Cataloging-in-Publication Data

McCormick Anita Louise.
    The Vietnam antiwar movement in American history / Anita Louise
McCormick.
        p. cm. — (In American history)
    Includes bibliographical references and index.
    Summary: Traces the history of the many protests staged by those in
opposition to the war in Vietnam and examines the legacy of this antiwar
movement.
    ISBN 0-7660-1295-6
    1. Vietnamese Conflict, 1961–1975—Protest movements—United
States Juvenile literature. 2. United States—History—1945–Juvenile
literature. [1. Vietnamese Conflict, 1961–1975—Protest movements.]
I. Title. II. Series.
DS559.62.U6M34 2000
959.704'3373—DC21
                                   99-37118
                                    CIP

Printed in the United States of America

10 9 8 7 6 5 4 3 2 1

To Our Readers: All Internet addresses in this book were active and appropriate
when we went to press. Any comments or suggestions can be sent by e-mail to
Comments@enslow.com or to the address on the back cover.

Illustration Credits: Department of Defense, p. 109; Enslow
Publishers, Inc., p. 17; Federal Bureau of Investigation, p. 67; Franke
Wolfe, LBJ Library Collection, p. 33; Library of Congress, pp. 9, 40, 64,
90; Michigan State Library, Special Collections, *American Radicalism
Vertical File*, <http://www.lib.msu.edu/spc/digital/msu.student.activism/
vietnamwarprotests.htm>, p. 38; National Archives, pp. 8, 14, 20, 39,
47, 50, 52, 88, 98, 101; National Park Service, p. 104; Reproduced from
the *Dictionary of American Portraits*, Published by Dover Publications,
Inc., in 1967, pp. 22, 79, 85; Yoichi R. Okamoto, LBJ Library
Collection, pp. 25, 27, 82.

Cover Illustration: Library of Congress; Reproduced from the
Dictionary of American Portraits, Published by Dover Publications, Inc.,
in 1967.

★ CONTENTS ★

THE KENT STATE SHOOTINGS

On May 4, 1970, a group of students gathered on the campus of Kent State University in Kent, Ohio, to protest the United States' involvement in the Vietnam War. They were upset over President Richard Nixon's recent decision to order American troops to bomb Cambodia, a southeast Asian nation that bordered Vietnam.

Nearby, nearly a hundred Ohio national guardsmen were observing the protesters. The National Guard had been called by Ohio's governor a few days earlier after a fire swept through the university's ROTC (Reserve Officers Training Corps) building. In the ROTC building, students were being recruited to join the military. Even though no one could prove who had started the fire, some authorities thought the protesters were responsible.

As the National Guard marched, several students started to throw rocks at the guardsmen and shouted, "Get out of here, get off our campus."[1] The National Guard used tear gas in an attempt to break up the crowd, but it did not work.

Kent State was just one of many protests against President Nixon's (right) escalation of the Vietnam War.

Then, without warning, the National Guard opened fire on a group of about two hundred protesters. Over sixty bullets whizzed through the air. The crowd panicked and ran in all directions.

Suzanne Madigan Irvin, a student who was attending the demonstration, said, "Suddenly, we heard what sounded like fireworks and in no time, a girl came running down the hill in front of us, with one shoe on and one shoe off. She was screaming and wailing, 'They've shot people, they've killed people' . . ."[2]

Tom Grace, a Kent State student who was injured during the incident, said:

I turned and started running as fast as I could. I don't think I got more than a step or two, and all of a sudden I was on the ground. . . . The bullet had entered my left heel and had literally knocked me off my feet. . . . It seems like the bullets were going within inches of my head. I can remember seeing people behind me, farther down the hill in the parking lot, dropping. I don't know if they were being hit by bullets or they were just hugging the ground. We know today that it only lasted thirteen seconds, but it seemed like it kept going and going and going. And I remember thinking, when is this going to stop? . . .[3]

The National Guard, called to the campus of Kent State to observe student protests, killed four students. The incident set off a wave of violent protest.

SOURCE DOCUMENT

I THINK AT SOME POINT, EVERYONE SAID, "ENOUGH'S ENOUGH." [BUT] I DON'T THINK THAT THE ANTI-WAR MOVEMENT REALLY TOOK HOLD UNTIL THE ADULT POPULATION JOINED IN. . . . AFTER THE SHOOTINGS, KENT BECAME SO WELL-KNOWN ACROSS THE COUNTRY. . . . WE WERE NO LEADERS OF A REVOLUTION, WE'RE JUST MIDDLE CLASS COLLEGE STUDENTS, TRYING TO GET AN EDUCATION LIKE EVERYBODY ELSE. BUT WE CARED ABOUT STUFF.[4]

Art Koushel, a student at Kent State at the time of the shootings, made this statement about the antiwar protesters and the reaction to Kent State.

When the Ohio National Guard finally stopped firing, four students had been killed and nine lay wounded. *Time* magazine reported that the campus of Kent State had been turned "into a bloodstained symbol of the rising student rebellion against the Nixon Administration and the war in Southeast Asia."[5]

For years, many people had questioned whether the United States should be playing such a large role in the Vietnam War. But after the Kent State shootings, all Americans were forced to look at the issues surrounding the Vietnam War—as well as the rights of those who chose to protest against it—more seriously than ever before.

THE VIETNAM WAR

The issues behind the Vietnam War were much more complicated than most Americans realized at the time. To most people in the United States, the war was being fought to prevent communism from spreading from North Vietnam into South Vietnam—and possibly into the rest of Indochina. But to many Vietnamese, the war was being waged to remove South Vietnam's corrupt government, which they felt had been unlawfully imposed on them by French officials.

France was interested in having colonies in Vietnam and other parts of Indochina because important natural resources such as rubber, tin, oil, and coal were plentiful there. Vietnam's battle to overthrow foreign rule was not new. It had been going on since the nation was taken over by France in the mid-1800s. But only when the United States became involved in the military struggle did the conflict in Vietnam gain the world's attention.

From the beginning, Vietnam sought independence from French rule, but it did not have the military strength to force the French to leave. However, isolated groups of Vietnamese soldiers, sometimes led by

Buddhist monks, staged numerous attacks on French colonial troops.

French commander Admiral Bonard made this report in 1862: "We have had enormous difficulties in enforcing our authority. . . . Rebel bands disturb the country everywhere. They appear from nowhere in large numbers, destroy everything and then disappear into nowhere."[1] This was known as a *guerrilla* war—meaning "little war" in Spanish.

Even after France had controlled Vietnam for decades, most French rulers had little respect for the people they governed. In 1905, Phan Chu Trinh, a former Vietnamese leader, made this statement to the French governor general:

> In your [French] papers, in your books, in your private conversations, there is displayed . . . the profound contempt with which you overwhelm us. In your eyes, we are savages, dumb brutes, incapable of distinguishing between good and evil . . . and it is sadness and shame that fills our hearts when we contemplate our humiliation.[2]

For several decades, no Vietnamese leader was able to organize a resistance movement strong enough to overthrow the French. Still, many people in Vietnam longed for the day when they would be free of the French, and once again permitted to govern themselves.

Ho Chi Minh

The leader of the resistance movement that eventually drove the French from Vietnam was Ho Chi Minh.

His name meant "He Who Enlightens." Ho was born in 1890. His father, Nguyen Sinh Huy, quit a government job because he did not want to serve the people who had invaded his country. When Ho was only nine years old, he carried secret messages for a revolutionary organization to which his father belonged. Later, Ho was expelled from school for trying to convince other students to turn against the French. After that, Ho traveled around the world and lived in England, France, Russia, and China. Still, he could not forget about the plight of Vietnam under French rule.

After World War I ended in 1918, Ho tried to present a petition for Vietnamese independence from France at an international peace conference, but the attempt was rejected. After that, Ho was unsure of what to do. He reached a turning point in his political thinking when he read "Thesis on the National and Colonial Question" by Vladimir Ilyich Lenin, the leader of Communist Russia. Ho decided that communism was the answer to his nation's problems. Communists believe that a government-run economy functions better than an economy run by private enterprise.

When Japan attacked Vietnam during World War II, Ho helped organize a resistance movement known as Viet Minh. Eventually, Ho's troops became a major force in driving the Japanese out of Vietnam. On September 2, 1945, Ho proclaimed the independence of the Democratic Republic of Vietnam. He then made a speech that was inspired by the American

Ho Chi Minh was the leader of the Communist forces throughout the Vietnam War.

Declaration of Independence: "All of the peoples of the earth are equal from birth, all the peoples have a right to live, to be happy and free. . . . Those are undeniable truths."[3]

Once Ho was in power, however, his government quickly became a dictatorship where people feared for their lives if they went against their leader's wishes. Opposing political parties were outlawed, and many of their leaders were jailed or killed. When elections were held, only Communist candidates approved by the government were allowed to run for office. Under Ho's government, newspapers and magazines could only publish articles that did not criticize government policy. Only music approved by the government could be played on the radio or performed in public. Loudspeakers on city corners blasted propaganda to the Vietnamese people.

Vietnam Is Divided

Ho's power was greatest in northern Vietnam, while much of southern Vietnam was still controlled by the French. In the years that followed, Ho's troops and the French government of South Vietnam were always at odds with each other. From 1945 until 1954, battles between the French-sponsored government and Communist resistance groups continued. Finally, in 1954, a conference was held in Geneva, Switzerland, to determine what to do about the situation in Vietnam. Delegates from North Vietnam, South Vietnam, France, England, the Soviet Union, Communist

China, and the United States decided to divide the nation temporarily at the 17th parallel of latitude. Ho's government would control the northern half of the nation and the government backed by France would control the southern half. As part of the agreement, called the Geneva Accords, French troops promised to leave North Vietnam immediately, and to pull out of South Vietnam as soon as possible. Vietnamese citizens were given three hundred days to move to whichever side of the 17th parallel they wished.

France agreed to withdraw its troops and set up a new, non-Communist government that would be run by Vietnamese leaders. Ngo Dinh Diem was chosen to be South Vietnam's new leader. South Vietnam promised to hold elections in 1956 to see whether their citizens wanted to reunite the country under one government. The United States promised to send economic aid to the South Vietnamese government.

Ho and his followers were not happy with this situation. Even though Vietnamese citizens had been appointed as leaders in South Vietnam, Ho believed they were taking orders from the American government, which had come into influence with the departure of the French in 1954. Ho's dream was to reunite the nation of Vietnam under a government that he controlled. By then, Ho had many supporters in South Vietnam. These rebels, who received weapons and support from North Vietnam, were known as the Vietcong. Before long, the opposing forces were fighting a civil war.

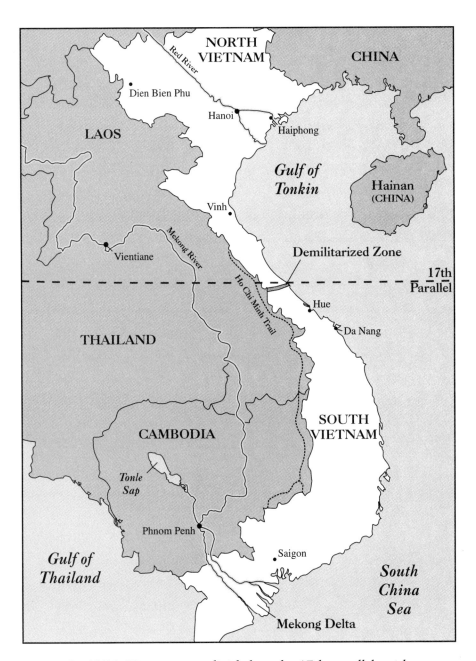

NORTH
VIETNAM

CHINA

Red River

Dien Bien Phu

Hanoi

Haiphong

LAOS

Gulf of
Tonkin

Hainan
(CHINA)

Vinh

Mekong River

Vientiane

Ho Chi Minh Trail

Demilitarized Zone

17th
Parallel

Hue

THAILAND

Da Nang

CAMBODIA

SOUTH
VIETNAM

Tonle
Sap

Phnom Penh

Gulf of
Thailand

Saigon

South
China
Sea

Mekong Delta

In 1954, Vietnam was divided at the 17th parallel, with
Communist forces ruling the north, and a non-Communist
government led by Ngo Dinh Diem ruling the south.

Americans Fear Communist Expansion

Because Ho was a Communist, the United States government was concerned about Vietnam. For years, Americans had worried about communism, believing Communists intended to take over the world and eliminate democratic governments. Many American national leaders at the time believed in the domino theory—if one government fell to communism, others in the same region were sure to follow. They felt that way because the Communist Soviet Union had taken control of several nations in Eastern Europe in the years after World War II. So when France needed help to protect this new South Vietnamese government from attacks by Ho's Communist troops, the United States government took an interest in the situation.

Before the Geneva Accords, President Dwight D. Eisenhower was not fully in agreement with France's having so much control in South Vietnam's government. Still, he believed that France was not just fighting to retake its former colony, but for the more important goal of stopping the spread of communism in Asia.[4]

In 1953, Eisenhower announced that the United States intended to "make substantial additional resources available to assist the French . . . in their military efforts to defeat the Communist Viet Minh aggression."[5]

Eisenhower raised the amount of American financial aid that South Vietnam was receiving from $10 million to $400 million per year. Eisenhower stated that this additional financial aid to South Vietnam was the least expensive way for the United States to stop the spread of communism and to preserve America's "ability to get certain things we need from the riches of the Indonisian [*sic*] territory, and from Southeast Asia."[6]

In addition to financial aid, Eisenhower sent American military advisors to help South Vietnam's army find a way to defeat Ho and the Vietcong rebels. However, Eisenhower saw the danger of allowing American troops to be involved in the actual fighting. He said, "If we were to put one combat soldier into Indo China [Vietnam], then our entire prestige would be at stake, not only in that area but throughout the world." He added, "I don't see any reason for American ground troops to be committed in Indo China."[7]

At first, only a few military advisors were sent. But even with their help, Communist forces were winning the war. So more advisors were sent. By the time Eisenhower left office in 1961, 675 American military advisors had been assigned to help the South Vietnamese government win the war.

Meanwhile, Ngo Dinh Diem's government was becoming even more corrupt. When Diem finally held elections in 1955, the results were rigged so that he would be certain to win. When the votes were counted, it appeared that almost 99 percent of South Vietnam's population supported him. Later, it was discovered that Diem had received more than two hundred thousand more votes in Saigon than there were registered voters in that city.[8]

The United States began its involvement in the Vietnam War with its leaders offering advice on the situation. In 1957, President Dwight D. Eisenhower (left) met with South Vietnam's President Ngo Dinh Diem (right).

David Hotham, a correspondent for the *London Times* and the *Economist*, wrote in 1959 that Diem

> has crushed all opposition of every kind, however anti-Communist it might be. He has been able to do this, simply and solely because of the massive dollar aid he has had from across the Pacific [the United States], which kept a man who, by all the laws of human and political affairs, would long ago have fallen. Diem's main supporters are to be found in North America, not in Free Vietnam. . . .[9]

Many American leaders, including President Eisenhower, realized that the South Vietnamese government was far from perfect. Under Diem, people who held differing views on religion and politics were often punished or killed. But the United States government saw Diem's regime as the lesser of the two evils and continued to send help.

This was a period when the United States was very confident about its role as a world leader. The nation's military power was at least as great as that of the Soviet Union. At the time, many people believed that part of the American role as a world leader was to prevent communism from spreading to other nations.

President Kennedy Faces the Vietnam Issue

When President John F. Kennedy took office in 1961, he was very concerned about the spread of communism. Only two weeks before Kennedy took office, Nikita Khrushchev, the leader of the Soviet Union, made an eight-hour speech in which he denounced the United States and promised to support Communist

John F. Kennedy continued extending aid to the South Vietnamese after he became president in 1961.

revolutions in all parts of the world.

In response to Khrushchev's comments, President Kennedy issued a warning in his inaugural address: "Let every nation know, whether it wishes us well or ill, that we shall pay any price, bear any burden, meet any hardship, support any friend, oppose any foe to assure the survival and success of liberty."[10]

In the early 1960s, most people in the United States knew little about Vietnam. They did not understand the issues that were causing a civil war in this Asian country, nearly nine thousand miles away. But at the time, many Americans felt that if communism were starting to spread, something should be done to stop it.

Even then, some of Kennedy's advisors were concerned that involvement in the Vietnam War could be very costly to the United States. Undersecretary of State George Ball warned Kennedy that America was heading for a full-scale war in Vietnam. Kennedy replied, "That's not going to happen."[11]

George Ball's prediction soon proved to be correct. By the end of 1963, sixteen thousand American advisors and soldiers had already been committed to help the South Vietnamese fight against Communist troops, known as the National Liberation Front (NLF), in South Vietnam.[12]

These military forces included people from the United States Army Special Forces, who were experts in jungle warfare. Many shipments of heavy weapons, tanks, and armored personnel carriers were also sent to Vietnam during Kennedy's administration.

But even with assistance from the United States, South Vietnam's leader, Ngo Dinh Diem, was rapidly losing the support of his own people. There was much corruption in his administration. Diem was also doing everything he could to force Buddhists to convert to Christianity. When he forbade Buddhists to fly religious flags during celebrations on May 8, 1963, protesters took to the street. Through that year, the number of protests increased, along with government brutality. Buddhist priests set themselves on fire in Saigon to protest that summer. Photographs of the incidents appeared in newspapers across the United States. By then, some Americans had already started to question what kind of government their tax dollars were supporting.

On November 2, 1963, Diem and his brother were assassinated by a band of rebel soldiers. During the next few years, the government of South Vietnam was in shambles as one group overthrew another. By the end of 1965, South Vietnam had gone through ten changes of leadership.

President Johnson Inherits the Vietnam War

On November 22, 1963, President Kennedy was assassinated, and Vice President Lyndon B. Johnson took over the office of president. Many people wondered what Johnson would do about the situation in Vietnam. Johnson had never shown much interest in foreign affairs. For a while, he concentrated mostly on his "Great Society" programs, designed to help lift poor Americans out of poverty. These programs included the Job Corps, Medicare, Medicaid, Head Start, and the Neighborhood Youth Corps.

But Johnson could not ignore Vietnam for long. On August 2, 1964, Johnson was informed that the American destroyer *Maddox* had come under attack. At the time, the *Maddox* was on a secret mission to observe South Vietnamese attacks on North Vietnam positions in the Gulf of Tonkin, off the coast of North Vietnam.

President Johnson warned North Vietnamese leaders that the United States would retaliate if there were any more attacks. Two nights later, the *Maddox* returned to the area, along with the destroyer *C. Turner Joy*. United States Navy officials saw some unusual signals on their radar screen and thought an enemy torpedo might be firing on them. However, no American ship or plane was hit. No one really knows what happened that night. But President Johnson felt

American troops in Vietnam greet President Lyndon B. Johnson and General William Westmoreland.

that North Vietnam had ignored his warning, leaving him with no choice but to take action against the North Vietnamese.

On August 4, 1964, President Johnson appeared on national television to inform the American public of his decision. He said, "My fellow Americans, hostile actions against United States ships . . . have today required me to order military forces of the United States to take action in reply. . . . Our response . . . will be limited. . . . We seek no wider war."[13] This action, which included bombing Vietnamese military targets from the air, signaled the beginning of the Vietnam War to most Americans.

The Tonkin Gulf Resolution

On August 7, President Johnson convinced Congress to pass a bill authorizing him to take all necessary measures to repel any armed attack against United States forces and to prevent further aggression. The bill also approved all necessary steps, including the use of armed force, if nations friendly to the United States asked for assistance. This was known as the Tonkin Gulf Resolution. It was passed by a 416 to 0 vote in the House of Representatives and by a vote of 88 to 2 in the Senate. Only Senator Wayne Morse of Oregon and Senator Ernest Gruening of Alaska voted against it. Explaining his vote, Gruening said, "All Vietnam is not worth the life of a single American boy."[14]

Despite the bill's overwhelming support in the House and Senate, some lawmakers were concerned about giving the president so much power. Normally, a president was required to go before Congress and gain approval before involving the nation in a war. After the resolution passed, only the president was in the position to make decisions about the United States' involvement in Vietnam—as well as any other nation that requested military help. And he could do that without an official declaration of war.

After the bill passed, Senator Morse said, "History will record that we have made a great mistake in subverting and circumventing the Constitution of the United States . . . by means of this resolution."[15]

Johnson Runs as the "Peace Candidate"

In the following months, President Johnson repeatedly claimed that he did not want to widen the war in Vietnam. In the 1964 presidential election, he portrayed himself as the "peace candidate" who wanted to end American involvement in Vietnam as quickly as possible. During his campaign, Johnson said, "We don't want our American boys to do the fighting for Asian boys. We are not going to send American boys nine or ten thousand miles away from home to do what Asian boys ought to be doing for themselves."[16] Johnson also ran commercials that caused many people to fear that

President Johnson (at right) meets with South Vietnamese President Nguyen Van Thieu in the hope of putting an end to the fighting.

his opponent, Republican Barry Goldwater, would involve the United States in a nuclear war with the Soviet Union if he were elected. That November, Johnson won the election by a landslide.

But Johnson did not keep his promise. Even before the election, Johnson had asked his advisors to make plans for a major air attack on North Vietnam.

During this time, President Johnson knew that the majority of people living in South Vietnam did not support their government. In 1965, Lieutenant Colonel John Paul Vann, who was regarded by many Washington officials as the most knowledgeable person on the situation in South Vietnam, stated:

> A popular political base for the Government of South Vietnam does not now exist. . . . The existing government is oriented towards the exploitation of the rural and lower class urban populations. It is, in fact, a continuation of the French colonial system of government with upper-class Vietnamese replacing the French. . . . The dissatisfaction of the agrarian population . . . is expressed largely through alliance with the NLF [National Liberation Front—also known as the Vietcong].[17]

America Becomes More Involved

On February 7, 1965, Communist Vietnamese troops made a surprise attack on an American military camp in the central highlands of Vietnam. Eight Americans were killed and 109 were wounded. Ten military airplanes were also destroyed. With the government as well as the military forces of South Vietnam on the verge of collapse, Johnson felt that the only way to save Vietnam from communism was to send more American soldiers. But now they were not only being sent as advisors. They were also engaging in battle.

As part of his plan, Johnson ordered B-52 bombers to make raids along North Vietnam's border with South Vietnam. This, he hoped, would cut off shipments of arms and other suppliers to Communist Vietnamese soldiers in the south. Later, he ordered constant bombing raids of North Vietnam in an operation known as Rolling Thunder, which lasted from March 1965 until late 1968. These bombing raids were very costly to the United States. During the raids, 818 airmen were killed and 918 military aircraft were shot down at a cost of more than $6 billion.

But no matter how many bombing attacks Johnson ordered, the Communist fighters did not back down. If anything, the attacks made them more determined to resist what they saw as another intruder trying to tell them how to run their country.

The Tet Offensive

On January 30, 1968, at the start of the Vietnamese New Year (known as Tet), about eighty thousand Communist troops and guerrilla fighters attacked more than a hundred cities and towns in South Vietnam. One group of Communist soldiers was able to force its way inside the United States Embassy in Saigon, South Vietnam. Other targets of the Tet attack included the South Vietnamese president's palace,

---

SOURCE DOCUMENT

TET-68 EXPLODED ALL THE OFFICIAL REASSURANCES THAT THE U.S. WAS WINNING THE WAR, THAT THE VIETCONG WERE ON THEIR WAY OUT, AND THAT THE WAR WOULD END SOON. TO MOST AMERICANS, TET CONFIRMED WHAT THEY ALREADY EXPECTED, THAT THE JOHNSON ADMINISTRATION HAD NOT BEEN TELLING THE TRUTH, THAT AMERICA HAD BECOME INVOLVED IN AN ENDLESS WAR THAT WAS CONSUMING EVER-RISING NUMBERS OF LIVES AND DOLLARS.[18]

Historian George Moss made this commentary about the American people's reaction to the Tet Offensive.

headquarters of the South Vietnamese Army, and a major Saigon airport.

The Tet incident came as a complete surprise to the United States military. No one had any idea that the Communist forces were capable of making such an attack. When American television news reporter Walter Cronkite heard what had happened, he exclaimed, "What . . . is going on? I thought we were winning the war."[19]

Once the assault was over, General William Westmoreland announced that 37,000 Communist troops and 2,500 American troops had been killed in the fighting. But even after enduring such staggering losses, the Communist troops in Vietnam were not ready to give up.

After the Tet incident, more people than ever believed that the United States should pull out of

Vietnam as quickly as possible. By that time, 53 percent of Americans believed that the government had made a mistake in sending American soldiers to fight in Vietnam.[20]

Frustration Builds

Everyone from President Johnson down to the lowest-ranking soldier was frustrated with the situation in Vietnam. Conventional warfare did not seem to be effective against the Communist soldiers, who seemed to come out of nowhere, attack, and then disappear into the jungle.

American soldiers in Vietnam constantly had to be on the lookout for surprise attacks and booby traps. They were frequently sent on search and destroy missions, in which they located a village controlled by Communists, burned it down, and moved on. Often, they could not tell the friendly Vietnamese from those who supported the enemy.

One lieutenant who was serving aboard the aircraft carrier U.S.S. *Constellation* said,

> We are going through the worst . . . flak in the history of man, and for what—to knock out some twelve-foot wooden bridge they can build back a couple of hours later. We can't hit the [Haiphong] docks where they unload the war material because we might hit the [Soviet] ships. . . . We've got a great big country with sophisticated equipment, trained pilots, expensive aircraft and . . . it's not worth the loss of planes or the loss of a single pilot. . . .[21]

Even when Johnson offered economic aid to North Vietnam in exchange for bringing an end to the fighting and keeping the country divided, Ho did not waver. To Ho, reuniting Vietnam under his leadership was far more important than any promises of peace or economic aid that the United States could offer.

Americans Begin to Oppose the War

As Johnson continued to send more money, soldiers, and weapons to South Vietnam, opposition began to grow. Some Americans were concerned that the bombing raids would provoke the Soviet Union or Communist China to step up military actions in the region.

Many people did not think it was right for so many young American men to be sent to a war in a small nation so far from America's shores. War had not been officially declared, yet more and more American resources were being sent into the conflict. Humanitarian groups voiced protests against the effect the bombing raids were having on unarmed Vietnamese citizens. As early as September 1963, the National Committee for a Sane Nuclear Policy called for the United States to end its involvement in Vietnam.

By the mid-1960s, even President Johnson's advisors were realizing that the tide of public opinion had begun to turn against Johnson on the Vietnam issue. On May 19, 1967, Secretary of Defense Robert S.

The war in Vietnam was given considerable media coverage, and Americans watched newscasts to keep up with the situation there. Press reports were not usually favorable for President Johnson or General William Westmoreland.

McNamara, who had originally been in favor of the war, sent President Johnson a memo that expressed serious concerns about the problems that continued involvement in the Vietnam War could cause:

> The Vietnam War is unpopular in this country. It is becoming increasingly unpopular as it escalates—causing more American casualties, more fear of its growing into a wider war . . . and more distress at the amount of suffering being visited on the noncombatants in Vietnam, South and North. Most Americans do not know how we got where we are, and most . . . are convinced that somehow we should not have gotten this deeply in. All want the war ended and expect their President to end it. . . .[22]

But despite growing opposition to the Vietnam War, American involvement continued to deepen. By the end of 1967, nearly half a million American soldiers were serving in Vietnam. Almost fifteen thousand Americans had been killed and more than one hundred thousand wounded. By then, involvement in the Vietnam War was costing the United States nearly forty thousand dollars a minute.[23]

As the United States government sent more American servicemen to Vietnam, antiwar protests spread rapidly across America. Marches, sit-ins, and other forms of protest began to take place at many colleges and universities.

THE ANTIWAR MOVEMENT

College students made up a majority of the protesters. But the antiwar movement included people from nearly every walk of life. Many college professors, businesspeople, parents of draft-age youth, religious leaders, doctors, lawyers, politicians, and entertainers also voiced their objections to American involvement in the Vietnam War.

Taking a Cue From the Civil Rights Movement

Many of the strategies used by antiwar demonstrators were inspired by activists in the civil rights movement that began in the South during the 1950s and 1960s. People across the nation had watched newscasts showing African Americans peacefully marching for the right to vote, to send their children to the same schools as whites, and to use the same public drinking fountains and rest rooms as white Americans. Despite opposition from law enforcement officials, African Americans were able to use peaceful protests as a method of winning equal rights.

One method of getting media attention that was first used during the civil rights movement was the sit-in. During civil rights sit-ins, protesters would sit at the table of a restaurant that discriminated against African-American customers until they were served. Many people who objected to American involvement in the Vietnam War held sit-ins at colleges, universities, and buildings that belonged to the military to bring media attention to the antiwar movement.

How Antiwar Groups Were Organized

The antiwar movement was not a single organization. It was made up of thousands of individual groups. Some groups were local; others had members all over the country. Some lasted for years; others staged only a demonstration or two.

Antiwar groups tried to attract as many members as possible. They accomplished this in a number of ways. According to author Melvin Small,

> . . . some Americans decided to join [the movement's] ranks because of grass-roots, door-to-door campaigning by individuals who tirelessly canvassed the neighborhoods and workplaces, while others were influenced by pamphlets, advertisements, and local lectures.[1]

Teach-ins were one important way to bring more people into the antiwar movement. During a teach-in, students, faculty members, and guest speakers discussed issues concerning the Vietnam War. The first teach-in took place on March 24, 1965, at the University of Michigan at Ann Arbor. More than three thousand people attended. During the spring of 1965, over one hundred teach-ins were held on college campuses across the United States. The largest teach-in took place at the University of California at Berkeley. More than thirty thousand people participated in the thirty-six-hour program.

Marching on Washington

In April 1965, the first major antiwar march on Washington, D.C., took place. It was organized by Students for a Democratic Society (SDS), a radical student antiwar group with branches at many colleges and universities across the country. At least twenty-five thousand people went to the nation's capital to let their elected officials know that they opposed American involvement in the Vietnam conflict.

Another major march on Washington by antiwar demonstrators took place on October 21, 1967. Approximately fifty thousand protesters appeared. Many of the participants were college students, but some older people also attended. A number of clergymen from various churches participated. The vast majority of the protesters were peaceful, but before the

Student Mobilization Committee
to End the War **NOW!**
invites you to a

VIETNAM TEACH-IN

Jan. 24 • 11:30 a.m. • 108B WELLS HALL

•SPEAKERS•

David Dellinger - CHICAGO CONSPIRACY 7
EDITOR LIBERATION

Martin Nicolsus - MOVEMENT ACTIVIST
SOCIALOGIST - WINNER 1969
ISAAC DEUTSCHER AWARD

Reese Erlich - OAKLAND CONSPIRACY 7
MOVEMENT ACTIVIST

John Donnohue - ASSOC. PROF. - ANTHROPOLOGY
MSU ADVISORY GROUP - VIETNAM

Mike Smith - EX DEFENSE ATTORNEY

•WORKSHOPS•
on
IMPERIALISM • RACISM • WOMEN'S
LIBERATION

•FILMS•

Several films on the war and the American
movement will be shown during the TEACH-IN

Students took on the task of educating others about what was happening in Vietnam by organizing discussions and "Teach-ins."

Growing tired of hearing of the loss of American soldiers in Vietnam, Americans took part in protests against the war.

march was over, approximately one hundred fifty people had been arrested.

Draft Evasion

For years, the United States government had used the selective service system, or draft, to determine which young men would be called to do military service. Men of draft age were required to fill out an application and carry a card to show they had registered for the draft.

During the Vietnam War, more young men refused to cooperate with the draft than at any other time in American history. To show their feelings toward the Vietnam War, many young men burned their draft cards, tore them up, or sent them back to the government. Destroying draft cards was against the law. But those who did it felt it was necessary to show the government how strongly committed they were to their beliefs.

In October 1965, David J. Miller set his draft card on fire on the steps of the draft office in New York City. Miller was one of the first to burn draft cards in public. Even though Miller spent two years in jail for his actions, he inspired many others to do the same thing.[2]

In the spring of 1966, students at Cornell University formed the first "We Won't Go!" group.

Young men of draft age protested the Vietnam War by publicly burning their draft cards.

One year later, draft resistance organizations had been formed on two dozen college campuses. In 1967, Stop the Draft Week activities were held in New York City and Oakland, California. Public draft card burnings occurred at many of these demonstrations. Antiwar activist Martin Jezer said,

> When the call for a massive draft card burning on April 15 [1967] arrived from the organizers at Cornell [University, New York State], I signed at once. I had no doubt that this is what I had to do. . . . Once imprisonment becomes an honorable alternative to the military, something to be sought rather than avoided, resistance to the draft can become massive. In order to strike at this fear, some of us will have to face imprisonment with joyous defiance.[3]

In March 1967, the Resistance, a national organization made up of people resisting the draft, was formed. Among its protests was a national draft-card turn-in, held in October 1967.

But there were ways other than outright defiance for young men to avoid being drafted. Some were able to get draft deferments, or postponements. Deferments could be obtained for a variety of reasons, including college attendance, medical conditions, or religious grounds.

Conscientious Objectors

During the Vietnam War, approximately one hundred seventy thousand young men were able to avoid the draft by proving that their religious beliefs did not permit them to kill. They were classified as conscientious objectors (CO), and were often required to do some type of alternative service. Any draft-age young man who wanted CO status had to fill out an application, then wait for the draft board to make its decision.

One young man who applied for CO status said:

> Within a month after my high school graduation, I found myself before my local draft board, appealing my I-A [eligible for the military] classification. I went by myself and I was real nervous. My whole future was riding on what those people thought about me. . . . A few weeks later, my father told me on the phone that a letter had arrived from the draft board. I asked him to open it and read it to me. The answer was yes. I got my CO. It was a very emotional moment for me, one of the benchmarks of my life. But my father made light of it, treating it with the same insignificance he had given the whole process.[4]

But not everyone who wanted CO status was able to get it. Members of churches known for opposing war, such as Quakers, Mennonites, and Brethren, were most likely to receive a CO status. People who were known to oppose the Vietnam War for political reasons had a more difficult time getting the exemption. In all, as many as three hundred thousand young men who applied for CO status were turned down.[5] Many who were not able to get CO status chose to flee the country or go to jail rather than join the military and possibly be sent to Vietnam.

Student Deferments

Attending college was another way to avoid the draft. College students were classified as 2-S, and their obligation to do military service was postponed until they had completed their education. In the later years of the Vietnam War, some college deferments were lifted, allowing students to be drafted. However, those college students who were sent to Vietnam were often given desk jobs that kept them in relatively safe areas.

James Fallows, who wrote of his experiences as a draft evader in *Washington Monthly* magazine, said,

> Ask anyone who went to college in those days how many of his classmates saw combat in Vietnam. Of my 1,200 classmates at Harvard, I know of only two, one of them a veteran who joined the class late. The records show another fifty-five in the reserves, the stateside army, or military service of some other kind. . . . See how that compares with the Memorial Roll from a public high school in a big city or a West Virginia hill town.[6]

During the Vietnam War, many African-American families did not have the money to send their sons to college. For that reason, African-American men stood a higher chance of being drafted and sent to Vietnam than white men.

Draft Resisters Flee the Country

Some young men who were not able to get deferments decided to leave the United States before they were drafted. During the course of the Vietnam War, approximately one hundred fifty thousand draft-age men made this choice. About eighty thousand draft resisters went to Canada, while others went to Sweden, Mexico, or other countries.

In many cities, especially in Canada and Sweden, draft resisters were able to find support from organizations composed of young people who had also fled the United States, as well as local sympathizers. These groups, along with books such as the *Manual for Draft-Age Immigrants to Canada*, tried to help draft resisters adjust to their new home.

Some parents were upset with their draft-age sons' decision to leave the country to avoid doing military service in Vietnam. But other parents were supportive. Derr, a young man who fled to Canada, said of his decision:

> I was living underground [in the United States] and working and really having a good time, except I didn't realize what was happening. I didn't realize the paranoia that was building [from living in fear as a fugitive]. Really, my parents were the first ones to voice what I had been thinking—about going to Canada. My parents brought it out in the open and said, "Look, you're getting no place here. Go start a new life. Live free. Don't live with this fear." And that's when I really decided to get going.[7]

Prosecution of Draft Evaders

One goal of draft resistance groups was to encourage so many young men to avoid the draft that the courts would be too crowded to prosecute them all. To some degree, they were successful.

During the Vietnam War, approximately 570,000 young men committed draft violations of one kind or another that could have sent them to prison for five years or more. However, less than half of these violations were reported to federal prosecutors. Out of that number, just twenty-five thousand were indicted and less than nine thousand were convicted. Some 3,250 young men were sent to prison for refusing to be drafted. Most were released in less than a year.[8]

The Counterculture

Many teenagers and young adults of the Vietnam era felt that their generation was different from any generation that had come before them. As a result, they created a new culture. It would become known as the counterculture.

The Vietnam War was one of the primary issues about which these young people were concerned. Members of the counterculture also questioned many things about the government and how society was run. They questioned the ideas and values that had been accepted by the generations before them. Distrustful of traditional politics, the younger generation believed in personal action and idealism, unlike their middle-class, conventional parents.

During this time, many young people started to let their hair grow long. They wore love beads and ragged blue jeans. They hoped to show that they held different beliefs and values from "the establishment," as they called the political and social systems created by the generations before theirs.

Many young people in the counterculture movement also experimented with marijuana, LSD, and other drugs. Still others turned away from the religious beliefs of their parents and followed spiritual teachers from India. The behavior of young people involved in the counterculture was often shocking to their elders. The differences in lifestyle between members of the counterculture and the older generations came to be known as the generation gap.

American Soldiers in Vietnam

Even with all the outcry against the Vietnam War, many young men felt they had no choice but to report for military duty. The American soldiers who were sent to Vietnam were younger than those who had served

---

SOURCE DOCUMENT

I WAS 19 YEARS OLD [WHEN I WENT TO WAR] AND I'D ALWAYS BEEN TOLD TO DO WHAT THE GROWN-UPS TOLD ME TO DO. . . . BUT NOW I TELL MY SONS, IF THE GOVERNMENT CALLS, TO GO, TO SERVE THEIR COUNTRY, BUT TO USE THEIR OWN JUDGMENT AT TIMES. . . . TO FORGET ABOUT AUTHORITY . . . TO USE THEIR OWN CONSCIENCE. I WISH SOMEBODY HAD TOLD ME THAT BEFORE I WENT TO VIETNAM.[9]

Veteran Charles Hutto explained his experience going to fight in Vietnam at a young age.

Though some young people did whatever they could to avoid the draft, others felt they had no choice but to serve.

in other wars in the twentieth century. The average age of a soldier drafted into the Vietnam War was nineteen. The average age of a soldier entering World War II was twenty-six.[10]

A survey taken by Notre Dame University found that 60 percent of draft-age men who were not sent into combat in Vietnam took some kind of action, such as obtaining a deferment or CO status, to keep themselves out of combat.[11] And many of the soldiers drafted to serve in the Vietnam War came from low-income to moderate-income families.

Most of the young men who were being drafted into the military during the early years of United States involvement in the Vietnam War had no idea what war was really about. Writer Albert Marrin said,

> They had been raised on World War II movies, particularly those of John Wayne. . . . In films like *The Sands of Iwo Jima*, he made war an adventure in which the good guys—our guys—were invincible. Americans always won, and did so accompanied by rousing music. Even when they died, death came quickly, neatly, painlessly. You never saw shattered bodies in a John Wayne movie.[12]

The young men who went to Vietnam quickly found that this conflict was like no war movie they had ever seen. Unlike the Hollywood version of a speedy American military victory, these young soldiers were exposed to the bloodshed and true horrors of a war that never seemed to end.

P eople on both sides of the Vietnam issue knew the media was a powerful tool in influencing public opinion in the United States. Television analyst Edward Jay Epstein said of the Vietnam era: "Never before in history has a nation allowed its citizens to view uncensored scenes of combat, destruction and atrocities in their living rooms, in living color. . . . [T]elevision, by showing the terrible truth of war, caused the disillusionment of Americans with the war. . . ."[1]

THE VIETNAM WAR IN THE MEDIA

The Credibility Gap

During the Vietnam War, Americans witnessed many troubling scenes on television. In 1965, a CBS news report showed a group of United States Marines using cigarette lighters to set fire to grass huts where Vietnamese families lived. The officer in charge said that he was under orders to burn the village down because Communist troops had been spotted there. CBS reporter Morley Safer said,

If there were Viet Cong in the hamlet, they were long gone. . . . The day's operation burned down one hundred fifty houses, wounded three women, killed one baby, wounded one marine, and netted four prisoners—four old men who could not answer questions put to them in English.[2]

To keep the public sympathy with him, President Johnson asked military leaders to issue progress reports. These reports gave facts and figures supporting Johnson's claim that Communist forces in Vietnam were finally being defeated. But when Americans watched the evening news, they heard a far different

Vietnam was the first war to be so heavily covered by the media. During 1968, CBS sent newscaster Walter Cronkite (at center, with microphone) and a camera crew to Vietnam to broadcast updates of the war to the United States.

story. Instead of the progress Johnson claimed to be making in the war, news reports revealed that ever-increasing numbers of American soldiers were being killed and wounded. Americans began to wonder whether they could trust the information their government gave them. This lack of faith in the government became known as the credibility gap.

By August 1967, newspaper correspondent James Deakin wrote, "the relationship between the President and the Washington press corps has settled into a pattern of chronic disbelief."[3]

The My Lai Massacre

In March 1968, a group of American soldiers was given orders to kill everyone in the village of My Lai in South Vietnam. They had been given this order because the military had received reports that some people in the village were helping the Communists. Even though no one from My Lai had fired a shot at the American soldiers, the soldiers herded the people of the village—mostly elderly men, women, and children—into a ditch and shot them with automatic rifles. Approximately four hundred people were killed. Only a few villagers were alive by the time a second group of American soldiers arrived and demanded that the killing be stopped.

Military officials were able to cover up the incident for longer than a year. But when the story of the tragic and unnecessary destruction of the Vietnamese village finally reached the press, many Americans were shocked.

Charles Hutto, an American soldier who participated in the My Lai massacre, said, "The impression I got was that we were to shoot everyone in the village . . . an order came down to destroy all of the food, kill all the animals and kill all the people . . . then the village was burned. . . . I didn't agree with the killings but we were ordered to do it."[4]

Press coverage of incidents like the My Lai massacre caused people to realize that the Vietnam War

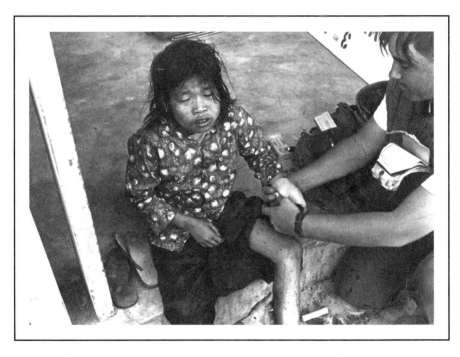

The media showed Americans that many Vietnamese people were having their lives destroyed by the war. Here, a young Vietnamese girl injured during the fighting in 1968 receives help.

was not only a battle against Communist soldiers. It also involved millions of ordinary Vietnamese people whose lives were being destroyed by the war. This, too, caused many Americans to question the Johnson administration's policy in the conflict.

Did the Media Go Far Enough?

Many people who opposed the war did not think television and the other media went far enough in exposing the true horror of the war. They did not feel enough was being done to ensure that statements made by the president and other government leaders were true. Journalist Jules Witcover said:

> In coverage of the war, the press corps' job narrowed down to three basic tasks—reporting what the government said, finding out whether it was true, and assessing whether the policy . . . worked. The group did a highly professional job on the first task. But it fell down on the second and third, and there is strong evidence the reason is too many reporters sought the answers in all three categories from the same basic source—the government.[5]

Antiwar Demonstrations in the News

Antiwar protests during the Vietnam era were often covered by the media. This was especially true of protests that attracted large crowds, became unruly, or clashed with the police. For that reason, some antiwar leaders tried to make their demonstrations exciting enough to catch the attention of the media. Radical antiwar leader Jerry Rubin once said:

Have you ever seen a boring demonstration on TV? Just being on TV makes it exciting. Even picket lines look breathtaking. Television creates myths bigger than reality.

Demonstrations last for hours, and most of that time nothing happens. After the demonstration we rush home for the 6 o'clock news. The drama review. TV packs all the action into two minutes—a commercial for the revolution.[6]

Underground Newspapers and Radio

But many people involved in the antiwar movement did not fully trust the reporters who worked for the major newspapers, radio, and television stations. So they set out to create alternate media of their own. With limited financial resources, they spread their opinions by means of leaflets, underground newspapers, and poster campaigns. Some of these alternative publications were the work of small groups of people. Others required the cooperation of thousands. By the time American involvement in the Vietnam War was at its peak, there were three national underground wire services, and over six hundred underground newspapers, with a total circulation of approximately 5 million. The *Liberation*, a journal and news service, was set up to help spread the message of the antiwar movement. It encouraged individuals to resist the war by withdrawing support from the government and society.

Some technically inclined people who opposed the war decided to put unlicensed "pirate" radio stations on the air to give antiwar protesters more of a voice than they had in the conventional media. Allan H. Weiner, a student at Lincoln High School in Yonkers, New York, was a leader in New York's underground radio movement. He helped create the Falling Star Network of pirate radio stations that operated out of homes and apartments in the New York City area. The network operated until August 12, 1971, when federal agents raided the stations and seized their equipment.

In his autobiography, Weiner wrote:

> The Falling Star Network was always the center of energy. . . . We always took lots of phone calls, both on and off the air. Doctors, lawyers, and people from all walks of life called up or came down to the stations to share their experiences with our listeners. . . . We got a lot of heavy calls from antiwar protesters, draft dodgers, and Students for a Democratic Society-type groups. Our network was a real unifying resource— which is one of the nice things that small, low-power community radio stations can do.[7]

Music of the Antiwar Movement

The antiwar movement did more than protest the Vietnam War through politics and the media. It also inspired a new kind of music. Bob Dylan; Joan Baez; Jimi Hendrix; Peter, Paul, and Mary; Phil Ochs; Arlo Guthrie; John Lennon; and other folk and rock singers captured the feelings of the protest movement with their songs. Their music also led people who had not yet taken a stand on the war to think more deeply about the issues involved.

Protest songs expressed the younger generation's dissatisfaction with society and government, and many offered hope for a better future. These songs promoted peace and racial harmony. They often questioned the goals and values of the government, as well as those of the older generation. While some protest songs had a general theme of dissatisfaction with the status quo, others focused directly on the Vietnam War. A writer for *Space City* magazine said, "music is responsible more than any other single factor in spreading the good news."[8]

Bob Dylan was one of the first popular musicians to write and sing protest songs, such as "Blowin' in the Wind," "Only a Pawn in Their Game," "The Times They Are a' Changin'," and "Chimes of Freedom," that were heard by national audiences. When asked about his lyrics, Dylan said,

> The idea came to me that you were betrayed by your silence. That all of us in America who didn't speak out were betrayed by our silence. Betrayed by the silence of the people in power. They refuse to look at what is happening. . . . They don't even care, that's the worst of it.[9]

Folk singer Phil Ochs was famous for the antiwar music he wrote and sang throughout the Vietnam era. In 1962, Ochs said, "Every newspaper headline is a potential song, and it is the role of an effective songwriter to pick out the material that has interest, significance and sometimes humor adaptable to music." In 1964, he released an album titled *All the News That's Fit to Sing.*[10] Ochs songs with an antiwar theme include "Talking Vietnam," "I Ain't Marching Anymore," and "Draft Dodger Rag."

At first, only a small number of radio stations were willing to play protest songs. Many station managers feared that songs with lyrics opposing United States military policies might anger many people. But as time went on and more people began to oppose involvement in Vietnam, station managers were no longer so worried about their audiences' reaction. Eventually, protest songs could be heard on many rock stations across the country. When Barry McGuire's antiwar song, "Eve of Destruction," was released in 1965, it became the most popular song in the nation.

In the late 1960s, three huge outdoor rock music festivals—the Be-In held at San Francisco's Golden Gate Park in 1967; the Monterey Pop Music Festival held in Monterey, California, in the summer of 1967; and the Woodstock Festival held in Bethel, New York, in 1969—provided a new way for people to come together. All these festivals attracted thousands of young people from across the nation.

Although these music festivals were not promoted as antiwar rallies, much of the music played there had themes of love, peace, and hope for a future without war. When Country Joe and the Fish came on stage at Woodstock to perform the anti–Vietnam War song,

"Fixin' to Die Rag," thousands of people got on their feet and sang along.

In the years since the Vietnam War, these enormous music festivals have been viewed with a great deal of nostalgia, both by those who were part of the antiwar movement during their youth, and by the younger generations. Woodstock, in particular, has come to be a symbol of the antiwar movement and its ideals. Today's young people have frequently tried to revive the spirit of the festivals that took place during the antiwar era with large outdoor musical concerts of their own.

During the mid-1960s, many government officials were forced to take a stand on the Vietnam issue. Those who supported the war effort were called hawks. Those who believed American troops should be brought home from Vietnam were known as doves.

THE NATION TAKES SIDES

In a 1967 article, Senator William Fulbright, a Democrat from Arkansas who wanted the United States to pull out of the war, said:

> While the country sickens for lack of moral leadership, a most remarkable younger generation has taken up the standard of American idealism. . . . The focus of their protest is the war in Vietnam. . . . They are demonstrating that, while their country is capable of acting falsely to itself, it cannot do so without internal disruption. . . .[1]

Hawks often felt that people who opposed the war were anti-American or even Communist. They believed that the United States military had to take a stand against communism, as it was doing in Vietnam, or else communism would spread throughout the world. Conservative Senator Barry Goldwater, who sided with the hawks, described his feelings about the peace demonstrations on college campuses by saying:

> The worth of educating our young people should be placed high above the antics of a few radicals—even in situations where those radicals might have a justifiable complaint in the scale of human values. The education of 20,000 students can never be weighed against the protest of a few hundred. . . . [W]hen a few hundred screaming Vietnam peaceniks run and shout over our college campuses they are distracting from the much more worthwhile endeavor of many thousands of students who are trying to learn what they need to know to become productive members of our society and leaders in our nation in the years ahead.[2]

Still, criticisms such as Goldwater's did not stop many Americans from taking a stand against the war.

Muhammad Ali Refuses to Be Drafted

Champion heavyweight boxer Muhammad Ali made news across the nation in 1967 when he refused to be drafted. At first, Ali did not think he would be called to serve in the Vietnam War. According to an intelligence test given by the army, his IQ [intelligence quotient] was only 78. Because of this low score, Ali was given a 1-Y draft status, meaning that he was unfit for military service. When this was reported on the news, Ali replied, "I only said I was the greatest. I never said I was the smartest."[3]

But many people had trouble believing that someone who had accomplished as much as Ali had was not intelligent enough to be drafted into the army. Democratic South Carolina Congressman L. Mendel Rivers was especially angry at the news. He declared that Ali's exemption was

> an insult to every mother's son serving in Vietnam. Here he is, smart enough to finish high school, write his kind of poetry, promote himself all over the world, make a million a year, drive around in red Cadillacs— and they say he's too dumb to tote a gun. Who's dumb enough to believe that?[4]

As United States involvement in the Vietnam War increased, the need for more soldiers grew. In February 1966, the army decided to lower the requirements for its intelligence test so that more men would pass. After this change, Ali became eligible for the draft. In April 1967, he was ordered to report for military service.

Ali believed that he should be exempt from service, both as a conscientious objector and because he was a Black Muslim minister. Black Muslims considered themselves a separate nation from the United States and did not feel they should be forced to take part in American wars.

The draft board did not agree with Ali's position. It denied Ali's request for an exemption. However, it did offer him a compromise. Instead of engaging in normal military duty, he could choose to be part of the Special Services—a branch of the military used to entertain the troops. As a member of the Special Services, Ali was told that he could fight in exhibition boxing matches and would not be required to carry a gun. Ali refused. He was so opposed to the Vietnam War that he preferred to risk up to five years in prison and a fine of up to several thousand dollars rather than taking the army up on its offer.

Ali made many public statements about his opposition to the Vietnam War. At one point, he issued a four-page statement to the press, explaining why his religious beliefs did not allow him to fight in the Vietnam War. He also wrote poetry about his stand against the war. One of his poems read:

> *Keep asking me, no matter how long*
> *On the war in Vietnam, I sing this song*
> *I ain't got no quarrel with the Viet Cong.*[5]

Even among African-American athletes, reaction to Ali's decision was mixed. Joe Louis, a well-known boxer, and Jackie Robinson, the first African American to play major-league baseball, felt that Ali's refusal to be drafted was wrong. But other African-American athletes, including basketball stars Bill Russell and Lew Alcindor (later known as Kareem Abdul-Jabbar), came out in support of Ali's decision.

While Ali was waiting for his case to be heard, the World Boxing Association and the New York State Athletic Commission decided to strip him of his title as world champion heavyweight boxer because he refused to serve in the military. His boxing license was also revoked. When the athletic commission's decision was announced, nationally known sports announcer Howard Cosell said, "It was an outrage, an absolute disgrace. Due process of law hadn't even begun."[6]

When Ali's case went to court in June 1967, the judge found him guilty of evading the draft. He sentenced Ali to five years in prison and a fine of $10,000. But Ali's lawyer appealed the case, and Ali was allowed to go free.

Three and a half years later, the United States Supreme Court overturned the lower court's decision. The Supreme Court ruled that Ali's refusal to do military service was based on his religious beliefs and was legitimate. After that, Ali was able to resume his boxing career.

Martin Luther King, Jr., Takes a Stand

On April 4, 1967, Martin Luther King, Jr., the famed civil rights leader, sharply criticized United States involvement in the Vietnam War for the first time. In a speech at the Riverside Church in New York City, King referred to the war as "madness." He also said that the United States was "the greatest purveyor of violence in the world today."[7]

King held a press conference in which he encouraged young people to resist the draft. He also announced that he had joined two important antiwar groups, CALCAV (Clergymen and Laymen Concerned About Vietnam) and Negotiations Now! Even though King had long been a pacifist and a low-key critic of the Vietnam War, his bold statements against American involvement in the Vietnam War made headline news. They instantly made him one of the most outspoken leaders of the antiwar movement.

Martin Luther King, Jr., the famous civil rights activist, became one of the most outspoken leaders to oppose the Vietnam War.

Some people involved in the civil rights movement feared that King's new focus on the Vietnam War would distract him from his goal of achieving equal rights for African Americans. They also feared that his stand against the Vietnam War would alienate him from President Johnson and other government officials who had sided with him on civil rights issues and worked to pass important legislation such as the Civil Rights Act of 1964.

Believing it was important for the United States government to end its involvement in Vietnam as quickly as possible, however, King persisted. He said to his critics, "I'm not going to sit by and see war escalated without saying anything about it. It is worthless to talk about integrating if there is no world to integrate in. The war in Vietnam must be stopped. There must be a negotiated settlement. . . ."[8]

During the mid-1960s, 40 percent of the combat troops in Vietnam were African-American. King charged that President Johnson was allowing such a large number of African-American men to be drafted simply because their families did not have the money to send them to college, which would have allowed them to obtain a deferment.[9]

King was also upset with the Johnson administration for allowing the Vietnam War to take so much money away from the "Great Society" programs that Johnson promoted to help the nation's poor. In a 1967 speech, King said:

> The promises of the Great Society have been shot down on the battlefields of Vietnam. The pursuit of this widened war has narrowed domestic welfare programs, making the poor white and Negro, bear the heaviest burdens. . . . It is estimated that we spend three hundred twenty-two thousand dollars for each enemy we kill, while we spend on the so-called War on Poverty only about fifty-three dollars for each person. . . . We must combine the fervor of the civil rights movement with the peace movement.[10]

John Lennon's Stand Against Vietnam

John Lennon, a former member of the British music group the Beatles also took a stand against the Vietnam War. After his marriage to Yoko Ono in

March 1969, the couple staged a press conference in their hotel room in Amsterdam, Holland, to call attention to the Vietnam issue. They sat in bed, wearing pajamas, for a week and answered questions from reporters. When asked why they decided on such a unique way of protesting the war, Lennon said:

> Protest for peace in any way, but peacefully, 'cause we think that peace is only got by peaceful methods, and that to fight the establishment with their own weapons is no good because they always win, and they've been winning for thousands of years. They know how to play the game of violence. But they don't know how to handle humor, and peaceful humor—and that's our message really.[11]

Two months later, Lennon and Ono staged a similar press conference in a hotel room in Montreal, Canada. During that conference, they introduced a new song called "Give Peace a Chance." It quickly became an anthem of the antiwar movement.

Author John Orman said,

> John [Lennon] and Yoko [Ono] invested much capital and time to promote a new product that they hoped would be popular on the market: peace. Lennon cared at a time when the antiwar movement and the youth movement for social justice needed some response from their cultural heroes.[12]

An Issue That Divided the Nation

By the late 1960s, many people wanted the war to be over as soon as possible. But even those who opposed United States involvement in the Vietnam War often

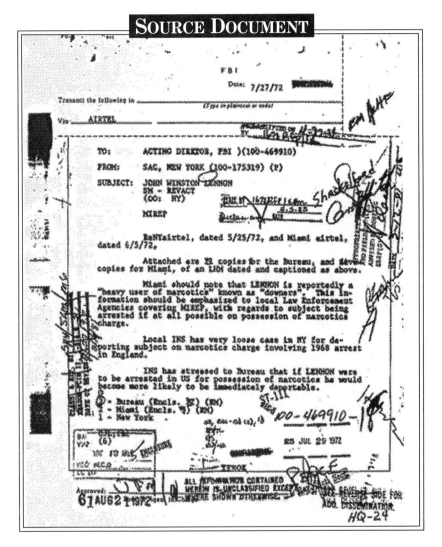

FBI

Date: 7/27/72

Transmit the following in _____
(Type in plaintext or code)

Via ___ AIRTEL

TO: ACTING DIRECTOR, FBI)(100-469910)

FROM: SAC, NEW YORK (100-175319) (P)

SUBJECT: JOHN WINSTON LENNON
             SM - REVACT
             (OO: NY)

             MIREP

             ReNYairtel, dated 5/25/72, and Miami airtel,
dated 6/5/72.

             Attached are 21 copies for the Bureau, and seven
copies for Miami, of an LHM dated and captioned as above.

             Miami should note that LENNON is reportedly a
"heavy user of narcotics" known as "downers". This information should be emphasized to local Law Enforcement
Agencies covering MIREP, with regards to subject being
arrested if at all possible on possession of narcotics
charge.

             Local INS has very loose case in NY for de-
porting subject on narcotics charge involving 1968 arrest
in England.

             INS has stressed to Bureau that if LENNON were
to be arrested in US for possession of narcotics he would
become more likely to be immediately deportable.

         2 - Bureau (Encls. 21) (RM)
         2 - Miami (Encls. 7) (RM)
         1 - New York

100-469910

25 JUL 29 1972

ALL INFORMATION CONTAINED
HEREIN IS UNCLASSIFIED EXCEPT
WHERE SHOWN OTHERWISE.

SEE REVERSE SIDE FOR
ADD. DISSEMINATOR.

HQ-24

*In an effort to end antiwar activism, the Federal
Bureau of Investigation and the Central Intelligence
Agency began to seek out those people who voiced their
opinions against the Vietnam War. Musician John
Lennon was a repeated target of the FBI, which kept a
file on the former Beatle and his antiwar activities.*

disagreed on how to end it. Some people felt antiwar demonstrations only served to prolong the war. The frequent protests proved to the North Vietnamese government that many United States citizens did not support the war. Some believed protests gave the North Vietnamese the motivation to continue fighting, knowing the enemy did not have enough support to continue fighting effectively.

Mark Arnold, a student at Oberlin College in Ohio, said in 1967:

> The only thing these demonstrations can accomplish is to prolong unduly the United States involvement in Vietnam because they provide the Viet Cong with one last desperate hope of victory. . . . Since the peace marches and sit-ins first began on a major scale in late 1963, there have been over 5,000 organized protests against the American involvement in Vietnam. Yet also since 1963, the total United States commitment has risen from a few thousand advisors to over 430,000 combat troops. . . . The demonstrations were hardly effective. . . .[13]

But others disagreed. Author Tom Wells wrote,

> The American movement against the Vietnam War was perhaps the most successful antiwar movement in history. It played a major role in restricting, de-escalating, and ending the war. . . . Had they [the antiwar protesters] not acted, the death and destruction . . . would have been immensely greater.[14]

Families Debate the Vietnam War

While some parents wanted their draft-age sons to stay out of the war if possible, others could not understand the unwillingness of the younger generation to fight when their government called. The parents of many student demonstrators had lived during World War II. They had lived during a time when communism and its expansion around the world was viewed as a very real threat to the United States.

However, the Vietnam War was different. During World War II, Germany and Japan were viewed as a clear threat to the well-being of the United States and its European allies. It was much more difficult, in the eyes of antiwar protesters, for the United States government to explain to the American public how North Vietnam could pose any threat to the country.

As opposition to the Vietnam War grew, government agencies were becoming increasingly concerned. The Federal Bureau of Investigation (FBI), Central Intelligence Agency (CIA), Department of Justice, and other government agencies were used in covert (secret) and sometimes illegal attacks against antiwar leaders.

6

THE GOVERNMENT CRACKS DOWN ON PROTESTERS

COINTELPRO

On October 28, 1968, the FBI launched a secret program known as the New Left COINTELPRO (Counterintelligence Program). It targeted antiwar groups the FBI felt were working to bring down or disrupt the United States government. The goal of COINTELPRO was to "expose, disrupt, misdirect, discredit or otherwise neutralize" organizations that opposed United States government policies on the war in Vietnam.[1]

FBI agents in COINTELPRO targeted every antiwar group and activist the government saw as a threat. As the first step of the investigation, COINTELPRO had FBI agents prepare reports about antiwar groups. Topics included how they were organized, who financed them, how many members they had, if they were under Communist influence, their political activities, religious beliefs, and whether they were likely to commit acts of violence. COINTELPRO was especially interested in monitoring antiwar groups that believed in destroying government buildings or using violence to achieve their goals.

One such organization was the Weathermen, an ultraradical group believed to have about four hundred members. In 1968, the Weathermen launched a campaign in Chicago called "Days of Rage." During the campaign, two hundred Weathermen and one hundred Weatherwomen marched down streets wearing helmets and carrying metal pipes. They broke windows and vandalized businesses. By the end of the demonstration, 290 of the demonstrators had been arrested.

The Weathermen were never able to gain enough members to hold large demonstrations. Eventually, many of the group's leaders became terrorists who were constantly on the run from the police. By the time the Vietnam War was over, the Weathermen had bombed nineteen induction centers, recruiting offices, and other government buildings across the nation.

But COINTELPRO also kept a close eye on peaceful antiwar demonstrations, photographing and trying to identify as many of the protesters as possible. When protesters were arrested, their names were immediately sent to FBI offices in their region.

Part of COINTELPRO's activities involved FBI agents printing and distributing materials that were intended to confuse and discourage antiwar protesters. COINTELPRO altered the dates of demonstrations and gave incorrect information on when buses would arrive to take people to demonstrations in distant cities, in an effort to prevent people from attending.

As part of the campaign against the antiwar movement, the FBI sent anonymous letters to the parents of students involved in protest activities. Often, the agent who wrote the letter pretended to be either a concerned friend who was interested in the student's welfare or the parent of a fellow student. One such letter read:

> Dear Mr. and Mrs. Jones,
> I feel you should be advised that your son, who is a fellow student . . . has recently become engrossed in activities which are not only detrimental to our country, our efforts in Vietnam and our common desire for justice, but are extremely detrimental to himself. Many of the people your son has been associated with are confirmed "Left Wingers" and some brazenly advocate communist ideology. While you may be somewhat unconcerned about your son's activities, I am sure you are cognizant of the fact that he is establishing for himself a stigma which soon he may not be able to erase. Although I would like to sign my name to this letter I do consider your son a friend of mine and would hate to lose his friendship. . . .[2]

Agents in COINTELPRO used letters to serve other goals, as well. Using fictitious names, they wrote to superintendents of schools where young people who had been involved in antiwar activities sought to get teaching jobs. The letters discouraged the school districts from hiring anyone who was such "a radical and trouble-maker."[3]

Antiwar Activists Strike Back

On March 8, 1971, a group of antiwar activists calling itself the Citizen's Commission to Investigate the FBI, broke into the FBI offices in Media, Pennsylvania, and found thousands of classified documents about COINTELPRO's activities. Copies of these documents were sent to congressmen who had spoken out against the Vietnam War, journalists, and newspapers such as *The Washington Post* and *The New York Times*.

Each mailing included a letter that explained why the group had broken into the FBI building. The letter said:

> We have taken this action because we believe that democracy can survive only in an order of justice, of an open society and public trust, because we believe that citizens have the right to scrutinize and control their own government and because we believe that the FBI has betrayed its democratic trust.[4]

In 1973, FBI Director Clarence M. Kelly defended COINTELPRO by declaring that the intent of the program was to "prevent dangerous acts against individuals, organizations and institutions—public and private—across the United States." He went on to say that the two thousand FBI employees in these programs "had acted in good faith and within the bounds of what was expected of them by the president, the attorney general, Congress, and, I believe, a majority of the American people."[5]

Still, many people felt that the FBI had gone too far in its investigations and harassment of antiwar activists.

The CIA Investigates Antiwar Activities

During the Vietnam War, President Johnson ordered the CIA to start a program called Operation Chaos to investigate antiwar activists. CIA agents in this program tapped phones, opened mail, and broke into the homes of people who were known to be active in the antiwar movement.

Historian Lawrence S. Wittner wrote, "The C.I.A. was soon maintaining files on 300,000 Americans, the F.B.I. on over a million. More military intelligence agents spied on American peace protesters than were employed in any other operation throughout the world."[6] But despite all the government's efforts to connect antiwar leaders with outside Communist influences, they were not able to find one case in which the North Vietnamese government sent money or gave orders to American antiwar groups.

North Vietnam Uses Celebrities to Help Stop the War

The Hanoi government, however, realized the power the American media had over public opinion. Truong

Nhu Tang, the North Vietnamese minister of justice, said that the American media "is easily open to suggestion and false information given by Communist agents. The [American] society is completely hypnotized by the media."[7] So the North Vietnamese looked for ways to make the American media work for their cause.

One way the Hanoi government influenced the media was to invite well-known American writers, entertainers, journalists, clergy members, and antiwar leaders to visit North Vietnam. The North Vietnamese showed these prominent Americans the damage that had been done by the United States military and talked about their desire to find some way of achieving a lasting peace.

In 1972, American actress Jane Fonda went on one of these tours. During her visit, she posed for photos on a North Vietnamese tank, which was used to shoot down American planes. She also made several broadcasts over Radio Hanoi. During these broadcasts, she told American pilots who flew bombing missions over Vietnam that they were no better than the war criminals who had served under German dictator Adolf Hitler during World War II. She also encouraged American military personnel to disobey orders given by their commanders. These actions were very unpopular. They earned Fonda the nickname "Hanoi Jane" among those who supported America's involvement in the Vietnam War.

By the late 1960s, the antiwar movement was at its peak. Marches against the Vietnam War were attracting more demonstrators than they had in previous years. Many protesters felt it would not be long before officials in Washington would finally be forced to bring American troops back home.

YEARS OF TURMOIL, 1968–1970

Eugene McCarthy and Robert Kennedy

Antiwar activists were pleased when Democrats Eugene McCarthy and Robert F. Kennedy, both of whom were running for president in 1968, voiced their opposition to continued involvement in the Vietnam War.

Eugene McCarthy, a United States senator from Minnesota, announced in November 1967 that he would challenge Lyndon Johnson for the Democratic nomination for president. Thousands of college students helped with McCarthy's campaign. They mailed out campaign literature, went door-to-door to talk to people, and made speeches on McCarthy's behalf.

To impress the voters, young McCarthy supporters stopped wearing hippie-style clothing and adopted a more conservative style of dress. Many young men who supported McCarthy cut their hair and shaved their beards. They called this "going clean for Gene." When the votes were counted in the New Hampshire primary, McCarthy had won 41.4 percent of the popular vote, and nine delegates to the Democratic National Convention. President Johnson, who won only three delegates, was stunned that so many people in his own party had rejected him.

Attorney General Robert F. Kennedy, brother of the late President John F. Kennedy, also received the support of many people who were opposed to the Vietnam War. In a speech on March 18, 1968, Kennedy said:

> I am concerned—as I believe most Americans are concerned—that the course we are following at the present time is deeply wrong. . . . [It] will not bring peace; will not stop the bloodshed; and will not advance the interests of the United States or the cause of peace in the world.
>
> The costs of the war's present course far outweigh anything we can reasonably hope to gain by it, for ourselves or for the people of Vietnam.[1]

President Johnson Decides Not to Run

On March 31, 1968, Johnson went on national television to say that he had decided to freeze the number of American soldiers being sent to Vietnam, to cut back on the bombing raids, and to start peace talks with the North Vietnamese government. Then he made an announcement that shocked the nation:

President Lyndon Johnson, who had led the nation through the early years of American involvement in Vietnam, decided not to run for re-election in 1968.

I shall not seek, and I will not accept, the nomination of my party for another term as your President. A house divided against itself . . . cannot stand. There is a division in the American house. I should not permit the Presidency to become involved in the . . . divisions that are developing.[2]

Johnson's announcement gave both Kennedy and McCarthy supporters reason to hope that their candidate could win the presidency and bring an end to American involvement in the Vietnam War.

Assassinations Shock the Nation

In 1968, two important antiwar leaders, Robert F. Kennedy and Martin Luther King, Jr., were assassinated. Some people in the antiwar movement believed that the government was secretly responsible. Even those who did not blame the government felt they no longer had the kind of leaders who could effectively work through the political system to bring an end to the war.

Carl Oglesby, a leader of Students for a Democratic Society, said:

Martin Luther King dead in April and just a couple months later Kennedy. What do you do? Go get a new hero and spend years teaching him and having the debates and doing the sit-ins . . . do it all over again while the people are dying in Vietnam? . . . That's why people started .talking about revolution, because reform [working within the system] had been made to seem like a dead-end street. How many times do you climb that tree just to have it chopped down beneath you?[3]

After the assassinations, some antiwar protesters became so frustrated with the situation that they turned to violent means of getting the government's attention. Their tactics included attempts to burn government buildings, stopping military trains, and fighting with the police.

The 1968 Democratic National Convention

When the Democratic National Convention opened in Chicago on Sunday, August 25, 1968, it soon became apparent that Hubert Humphrey, who served as vice president under Johnson, would be selected as the Democratic candidate for president. Party leaders did not want the national television audience to see how divided the Democratic party was, so Eugene McCarthy's supporters were not even permitted to bring banners or signs into the convention hall.

When McCarthy's delegates attempted to address the convention, their microphones were cut off. Inside the convention hall, they began chanting, "Stop the war! Stop the war!" Fights broke out between delegates, but the police arrested only delegates who supported McCarthy. Even news reporters were threatened and beaten. After that, some antiwar protesters were so angry that they found every way possible to disrupt the convention.

During the convention, thousands of demonstrators gathered in streets and parks throughout Chicago. The mayor of Chicago, Richard Daley, ordered the police to disperse the protesters. When the police could not

Senators William Fulbright (left) and Eugene McCarthy (right) were opposed to keeping American soldiers in Vietnam. They became popular with antiwar activists, especially young people, who campaigned for McCarthy in the presidential election of 1968.

successfully break up the demonstration, the National Guard was brought in to deal with the situation.

Three days after the start of the convention, about five thousand antiwar demonstrators began to march toward the building where the Democratic National Convention was being held. Suddenly, the Chicago police ran into the crowd, swinging their clubs at anyone they could hit. Then the police charged a group of McCarthy campaign workers who were standing near a hotel. The police forced the campaign workers back against the hotel's window until the glass broke, injuring many of them. The incident at the convention became known as Bloody Wednesday.

Pulitzer Prize–winning author Norman Mailer described the antiwar demonstrators at the 1968 Democratic National Convention:

> They were young men who were not going to Vietnam. So they would show every lover of war in Vietnam that the reason they did not go was not for lack of courage to fight; no, they would carry the fight over every street . . . where the opportunity presented itself. If they had been gassed and beaten, their leaders arrested on fake charges . . . they were going to demonstrate that they would not give up, that they were the stuff out of which the very best soldiers were made. . . . It seemed as if the more they were beaten and tear-gassed, the more they rallied back.[4]

When the convention was over, Vice President Hubert H. Humphrey had been nominated as the Democratic candidate for president. Despite all the clashes between antiwar protesters and law enforcement officials in the streets, the courts were able to charge only eight demonstrators with trying to start a riot. Later, investigators found that the police, not the demonstrators, had caused most of the violence at the convention.

However, the Democratic National Convention of 1968 left many people in the antiwar movement feeling as though they had nowhere to turn in the political system. One protester said: "In Chicago, I concluded that everything I had been taught about the American political system was false. There was no democracy when it came to the war. . . . And dissent was going to meet with state violence. It was horribly disillusioning."[5]

Nixon and Humphrey Promise to End the War

By the time of the 1968 presidential campaign, the majority of Americans wanted the war in Vietnam to end as soon as possible. But they disagreed strongly about how that goal should be accomplished. Doves wanted the United States government to bring all American troops home as soon as possible, regardless of how the war would end in their absence. Hawks, on the other hand, wanted the United States military to defeat the Communist forces in Vietnam quickly by dropping even more bombs. Both Republican presidential candidate Richard Nixon and Democratic candidate Hubert Humphrey claimed to have a plan to end American involvement in the Vietnam War in a way that would not humiliate the United States in the eyes of the world. Neither candidate, however, would reveal his plan to the American public.

In November 1968, Nixon defeated Humphrey by a narrow margin. For a time after Nixon took office, antiwar groups did not stage as many protests as they had earlier. They waited to see what Nixon would do.

Vietnamization

On June 8, 1969, Nixon announced his plan to end United States involvement in the Vietnam War. This plan, known as Vietnamization, was to end American involvement in the war by equipping the South Vietnamese better to fight their own battles. As part of this plan, Nixon announced that he would immediately bring twenty-five thousand soldiers home from Vietnam. The rest would be brought home gradually, as South Vietnamese soldiers were trained to replace them.

People who were opposed to the Vietnam War were glad to hear that American soldiers would soon be coming home. At the same time, however, the morale and discipline among the troops who were left to fight in Vietnam collapsed. Many soldiers had nearly given up on the possibility of winning the war. Their main goal was to stay alive until the government let them return home.

Richard Nixon was elected president in 1968. The major goal of his presidency would be to end the Vietnam War.

A much higher percentage of American military personnel than usual went AWOL (absent without leave) during this period. Desertions were also on the increase. The number of army desertions rose from 27,000 in 1967 to 76,634 in 1970, or fifty-two desertions per thousand soldiers. The marines also reported a high desertion rate—sixty per one thousand men.[6]

Incidents of soldiers fragging, or killing, an officer who ordered them into dangerous situations also increased dramatically. Although no one can be sure how many officers were killed by the men they commanded, the Defense Department estimates that 788 fraggings took place in Vietnam between 1969 and 1972.[7]

Many government officials, as well as antiwar groups and former Vietnam soldiers, urged President Nixon to set definite dates by which all American soldiers would be removed from Vietnam. Many antiwar demonstrations were held in the fall of 1969. But Nixon still believed that the majority of Americans felt it was more important to continue to fight the spread of communism than to bring the Vietnam War quickly to a close.

Invasion of Cambodia

On April 30, 1970, Nixon announced that American troops had invaded Cambodia, a nation to the west of Vietnam, through which North Vietnam was transporting troops and supplies. Nixon believed that his actions would weaken North Vietnam's army to the point that the war would soon end. But many Americans were angry because Nixon's strategy would expand the war into even more of Indochina. Joe Urgo, who lived in New York at the time, said,

> It was something I'd never ever seen before and never seen since. I could feel the polarization. . . . On that day or two after the Cambodian invasion, this whole city was filled with thousands of people all over the streets debating. You could just go from group to group arguing.[8]

As a response to Nixon's decision to invade Cambodia, antiwar activists held huge peace demonstrations at hundreds of universities and colleges. More people than ever were coming out to demonstrate against American involvement in the Vietnam War.

By the spring of 1970, some protesters had given up on peaceful demonstrations. They turned to violent clashes with the police and set fire to buildings that belonged to branches of the military. Government leaders were so concerned about the situation that they ordered the National Guard to university campuses in several states to restore order. On May 4, 1970, the nation was shocked to learn that the National Guard had opened fire on a group of students protesting against the war at Kent State University in Ohio, killing four and wounding nine student protesters.

But even this tragic event did not dampen the spirit of the antiwar movement. Instead, demonstrations became larger and more frequent. One day after the

President Nixon held press conferences concerning the war to help appease Americans, who had come to distrust their leaders on the Vietnam issue.

Kent State shootings occurred, over two hundred colleges and universities were closed due to protests. One week later, over four hundred colleges and universities were forced to shut down. Author Tom Wells wrote:

> [I]t wasn't [just] the students, professors, and administrators who were up in arms in May [1970, just after Kent State]. Other Americans were demonstrating in city after city and town after town across the country. Mass rallies were held in many places. GIs [soldiers] protested at a dozen military bases, some of which had no previous history of dissent. Clergy, doctors, lawyers, editors, and other professionals flooded into Washington to express their opposition to the war and domestic government violence.[9]

Local government officials reacted to these protests in a variety of ways. Martial law was declared in several college towns. In some instances, curfews were imposed. In others, the state police were brought in to restore order. But despite everything government officials did, the protesters could not be silenced.

Peace Protests in Washington

On the weekend of May 9 and 10, 1970, antiwar groups from across the nation held a huge demonstration in Washington, D.C. They wanted President Nixon to see how angry they were over the expansion of the Vietnam War into Cambodia. They also wanted to prove to the government that even the Kent State shootings would not stop them from standing up for their beliefs.

Usually, organizations that wanted to demonstrate or hold a rally on federal land were required to apply for a permit at least two weeks in advance. But with the nation's anger building, Washington officials decided to waive that requirement and allow the antiwar protesters to demonstrate without a permit.

The antiwar demonstration held that weekend was one of the largest in the nation's history. Over one hundred thousand people came to Washington by car, bus, train, and airplane to let government officials

During Richard Nixon's presidency, thousands of people of all ages gathered in Washington, D.C., to show their opposition to American involvement in the Vietnam War.

know they were tired of the way the Vietnam War was being handled. But even though the rally was well attended, the hot and humid weather, problems with amplifiers, and speeches by political leaders who seemed to have no solutions to the crisis in Vietnam made it a disappointing experience for many who had come to demonstrate.

Even more disappointing was Nixon's response. He told the American public that he viewed the demonstrators as extremists who did not appreciate the sacrifices soldiers were making to protect the world from communism. Then he ordered the largest bombing attacks on Vietnam and Cambodia since he had taken office.

But the tide of public opinion was starting to turn against Nixon. Even people in high government positions were beginning to realize that Nixon's plan to end the Vietnam War was not working. William Fulbright, chairman of the Senate Committee on Foreign Relations, denounced Nixon's expansion of the Vietnam War into Cambodia. Fourteen other members of the United States Senate demanded that Nixon immediately call for a cease-fire in Vietnam.

Finding a Way Out

By the early 1970s, it seemed clear that the United States could not help South Vietnam win the war unless massive amounts of supplies and many more American troops were sent to Vietnam. Government officials debated what to do. The majority of

Americans were tired of the war. They did not feel a victory against North Vietnam was worth the additional American lives or money it would cost. In a poll taken during 1970, two thirds of Americans wanted the government to bring all United States soldiers back home, even if that meant Communists would take over South Vietnam.[10]

In the summer of 1970, President Nixon said:

> I know that all Americans are tired of the war in Southeast Asia. . . . But I believe that most Americans would like to extricate ourselves in a manner which will encourage a stable peace. We should not leave a vacuum to be filled by Communist. . . . I am convinced that the Cambodian operation has helped hasten Vietnamization and has helped to ensure its success.[11]

Many Americans believed that Nixon's plan had a chance of working, and the number of antiwar demonstrations decreased for a time. But others felt Nixon was only using the idea of Vietnamization as a way to keep down protests while American involvement in the conflict continued.

Commission on Campus Unrest

Because of all the conflict over the Vietnam War, Nixon decided to appoint a committee to study what had happened at Kent State, as well as at other colleges and universities across the nation. It was known as the President's Commission on Campus Unrest. After studying the issue for ninety days, the committee, headed by William Scranton, former Republican governor of Pennsylvania, released its findings.

The committee's report said that disagreeing with the government is not a crime. However, committing acts of violence, such as burning or bombing buildings, as some antiwar protesters had done, was against the law. The committee also felt it was Nixon's responsibility to make more of an effort to bring the nation together. One way the committee believed the president could help the situation was to pay attention to what antiwar protesters had to say.

Secretary of the Interior Walter Hickel also believed President Nixon should pay more attention to the antiwar protesters. He wrote Nixon a letter that said:

> About 200 years ago, [England] . . . found itself with a colony [the American colonies that became the United States] in violent protest by its youth. . . . Their protests fell on deaf ears, and finally led to war. The outcome is history. If we read history, it clearly shows that youth in its protest must be heard.[12]

By the early 1970s, President Nixon realized that the Vietnam War could not drag on forever. In 1971, Nixon asked Henry Kissinger, the national security advisor, to start holding peace talks with the leaders of North Vietnam and South Vietnam. Nixon also opened relations with China and the Soviet Union in the hopes that those nations would encourage North Vietnam to sign a peace agreement. But ending the war through peace talks was not easy. Even when a deal was reached with North Vietnam, South Vietnam's leaders refused to sign it.

8

THE VIETNAM WAR DRAWS TO A CLOSE

The Pentagon Papers

In 1971, Daniel Ellsberg, who had been a Defense Department advisor to four presidents, decided to release a seven-thousand-page Defense Department study about the Vietnam War to the press. This document, known as the Pentagon Papers, told the real story of the Vietnam War. It exposed government lies and deceptions, many of which took place during the Johnson administration. Excerpts from the Pentagon Papers were published in *The New York Times* and *The Washington Post*. The complete document was also published as a book.

When asked why he decided to release the documents, Ellsberg said, "It was something . . . that I thought had to be done. . . . To do less would be wrong."[1] After the Pentagon Papers were released, many people were more convinced than ever that America's involvement in the war must end.

Ellsberg was arrested for espionage. However, the judge dismissed the case and found Ellsberg not guilty of all charges.

Vietnam Veterans Against the War

On April 30, 1971, approximately two thousand members of an antiwar organization called Vietnam Veterans Against the War held a demonstration in Washington, D.C. Many of the demonstrators had lost arms or legs in the fighting and were confined to wheelchairs. The veterans went to the steps of the Capitol, shouted out their names and ranks, and expressed their grievances against the war as they threw down the Congressional Medals of Honor they had won in combat.

Peace Talks

During his 1972 presidential campaign, Nixon assured voters that peace was at hand. Many antiwar protesters

SOURCE DOCUMENT

THE MASSIVE CIVIL DISOBEDIENCE AGAINST THE VIETNAM WAR—BY MEN IN THE MILITARY, BY DRAFTEES, AND BY CIVILIANS—CANNOT BE JUSTIFIED SIMPLY BECAUSE IT WAS CIVIL DISOBEDIENCE, BUT BECAUSE IT WAS DISOBEDIENCE ON BEHALF OF A HUMAN RIGHT—THE RIGHT OF MILLIONS OF PEOPLE IN VIETNAM NOT TO BE KILLED BECAUSE THE UNITED STATES SAW IN SOUTHEAST ASIA (AS PRESIDENT JOHN F. KENNEDY PUT IT), "AN IMPORTANT PIECE OF REAL ESTATE."[2]

Historian Howard Zinn made this statement about the antiwar movement as a struggle for human rights.

did not believe him and gave their support to Democratic Senator George McGovern, who took an antiwar stand. But even with the controversy over the Vietnam War, Nixon was able to win the election by a landslide.

On January 21, 1973, the day Nixon was inaugurated to his second term as president, a major protest against the Vietnam War took place in Washington, D.C. Even though peace talks were going on at the time, protesters wanted to make sure that the Nixon administration knew how strongly they felt on the issue.

After a few more months of negotiating with the Vietnamese, a deal was finally reached. On January 27, 1973, the Paris Peace Accords—also known as the Agreement on Ending the War and Restoring Peace in Vietnam—were signed. Nixon proclaimed, "We have finally achieved peace with honor."[3]

Once the agreement was signed, American troops were no longer directly involved in the fighting. Both sides released their prisoners of war. But even after the United States was no longer involved, approximately nine thousand American civilians remained in Vietnam as advisors. Most of these men employed by the South Vietnamese government.

But the Vietnam War was not yet over. Shortly after the agreement was signed, both sides began violating the peace agreement and sending soldiers into each other's territory.

In January 1973, Henry Kissinger (seated at center) signed the Paris Peace Accords, which finally ended United States involvement in the Vietnam War.

Congress Cuts Off Funds for the War

By the middle of 1973, Nixon's popularity had been heavily damaged by the Watergate scandal, in which his administration was found to have conducted illegal campaign activities. This compromised his ability to push the programs he wanted through Congress. That summer, a law that would prevent Nixon from sending any more money to assist in the conflict in Vietnam was making its way through Congress. The War Powers Act, also known as the Fulbright-Aiken Amendment, said:

> Notwithstanding any other provision of law, on or after August 15, 1973, no funds herein or heretofore appropriated may be obligated or expended to finance directly or indirectly combat activities by United States military forces in or over or from off the shores of North Vietnam, South Vietnam, Laos or Cambodia.[4]

On July 1, 1973, the amendment became law. Now Congress, rather than the president alone, would have the power to determine what actions could be taken in the Vietnam War. When President Nixon resigned from office as a result of the Watergate scandal in August 1974, Congress had a new president—Gerald Ford—with whom to deal on the issue of Vietnam.

The Fall of Saigon

With the United States military no longer assisting in the war effort, Communist troops from North Vietnam took the opportunity to gain more territory.

In early April 1975, North Vietnamese troops had advanced so far into South Vietnam that President Ford begged Congress to grant more than $700 million in military aid to prevent South Vietnam from falling to the Communists. But Congress knew that the American public had grown tired of the war and refused to provide any additional aid to the South Vietnamese government.

On April 30, 1975, North Vietnamese troops took over Saigon, the capital of South Vietnam. Until the last possible minute, United States military helicopters used the roof of the American Embassy to evacuate people from the country.

After the North Vietnamese took over South Vietnam, thousands of South Vietnamese who had worked for the United States or the South Vietnamese government were sent to Communist reeducation camps. Many of these camps were used as prisons, while others were used as retraining centers for work that needed to be done under the new Communist government. Living conditions in the reeducation camps were harsh, and many South Vietnamese prisoners became ill and died there.

The Devastation of Vietnam

The Vietnam War took a heavy toll on Vietnamese civilians. A United States Senate subcommittee on refugees estimated that 400,000 South Vietnamese civilians were killed, 900,000 were wounded, and 6.5 million became refugees because of the fighting.[5] It is

When the North Vietnamese invaded South Vietnam after the end of the war, many refugees fled the country to avoid the Communist takeover.

likely that North Vietnam had nearly the same number of casualties.

Many cities and towns in both North and South Vietnam were severely damaged by the war. Numerous small villages were completely destroyed. Roads and bridges throughout Vietnam were heavily damaged by bombs.

Vietnam's environment was badly damaged as well. During the war, foliage-destroying chemicals, such as Agent Orange, were sprayed on about 12 percent of South Vietnam's land. These chemical sprays, used to defoliate trees and make Communist troops easier to locate, also destroyed important crops and contaminated the soil, making it impossible for many farmers to grow food. Flooding was also a problem in areas where trees had been destroyed.

In addition to the problems Agent Orange caused to the environment, people who came in contact with it often suffered from serious health problems. Many American soldiers who served in Vietnam had health problems for years after they returned home. The cancer rate of people living in areas that had been sprayed with Agent Orange skyrocketed. Stillborn babies and babies with serious birth defects were common.

In some parts of Vietnam, the earth was turned upside down by explosives. Bombs and mines had blown fertile topsoil away and left fragments of rock in its place. Farmers always had to be on guard for unexploded mines or shells that could kill or maim them.

The Cost of the Vietnam War

United States involvement in the Vietnam War was very costly to the nation, both in lives and in dollars. A total of 2.8 million American men saw military service during the Vietnam War. Approximately 51,000 were killed. Another 270,000 were wounded—21,000 of those severely enough to be classified as disabled veterans. Another 1,400 American soldiers were reported missing in action.[6] The total cost of the Vietnam War was more than $106 billion. That figure does not include the cost of benefits to veterans who served in the military during the Vietnam War.

Once the conflict was over, many Americans had trouble understanding why the United States had been unable to defeat such a small nation whose technology lagged far behind its own. The war caused many people to question their belief that the United States could conquer any enemy. Author Loren Baritz wrote:

> We lost the war because we were never clear about the guerrillas, their popular support, the North Vietnamese, or ourselves. Our marvelously clever technology did not help us to understand the war and, in fact, confused us even more because it created our unquestioning faith in our own power.[7]

President Carter Pardons Draft Evaders

When President Jimmy Carter took office in 1977, one of his first actions was to grant an official pardon to anyone who had evaded the draft during the Vietnam War. That meant that every man who had left the country to avoid military service could come home without fear of being arrested.

Carter said, "I think it is time for the damage, hatred, and divisiveness caused by the Vietnam War to be over."[8] He also called for the Defense Department to reevaluate the cases of 432,000 servicemen who had been given less than honorable discharges. That gave these veterans the opportunity to present their cases and possibly become eligible for benefits that are only available to honorably discharged veterans.

The Vietnam Veterans Memorial was dedicated in 1982. The monument, which contains the names of the thousands who died or were missing in the war, was one attempt to heal the scars left by Vietnam.

Many Americans cheered Carter's decision. They felt it was time for the nation to heal the wounds caused by the Vietnam controversy and move on. But others were appalled. Senator Barry Goldwater declared that Carter's pardon of draft evaders was the "most disgraceful thing that a President has ever done."[9]

Attempting to Heal the Scars of the War

Several years later, another attempt was made to heal the scars left by division over the Vietnam War. The Vietnam Veterans Memorial dedication ceremony was held in Washington, D.C., in November 1982. The names of the thousands of Americans who died in the Vietnam War or were missing in action were engraved on a monument and displayed to the public. Veterans, families of the dead, and those who had protested the war all attended the ceremony. Author Stanley Karnow wrote:

> From afar, the crowds resembled the demonstrators who had stormed the capital during the Vietnam War to denounce the conflict. But past controversies were conspicuously absent this weekend. Now Americans appeared to be redeeming a debt to the men who had fought and died. . . . The faces, the words of dedication, and the monument itself seemed to heal wounds.[10]

The Vietnam War left many Americans with a distrust of the government that they had never before experienced. If the government could have such poor judgment about sending so many Americans to die in an unwinnable foreign war, what else could it be wrong about? If government officials could lie to the public about how the war was going, what other secrets might they be keeping?

LEGACY OF THE ANTIWAR MOVEMENT

Sam Brown, who attended college during the Vietnam era, said:

> For those of us who actively dissented [protested], the war has been the point around which we pivoted our lives during the last decade. It shaped our attitudes and personal lives more than we ever imagined. Some of us had to overcome a deep suspicion and at times the justified paranoia that those in authority were systematically disrupting our lives. . . . A few of us "burnt out" and rejected everything about the political process. . . . But many more of us [had] a positive commitment to make government more responsive to people where they live and work, at the local and state level.[1]

No More Vietnams

After the Vietnam War was over, many who had opposed the conflict found other peace-related causes to support. Some joined groups that demonstrated against the buildup of nuclear weapons. They hoped to influence the government not to spend so much tax money on weapons.

For years after the end of the war, Americans showed an intense fear of becoming engaged in a similar unsuccessful conflict. Whenever trouble erupted, many protested the idea of United States involvement. For example, when United States armed forces were sent to help ease tensions in Grenada in 1983, the persistent cry of "No More Vietnams" showed the American people's reluctance to become involved in an unwinnable war once again.

When Iraq invaded Kuwait in 1991, military personnel from the United States and other United Nations countries worked together to force Iraq's army out of Kuwait. President George Bush assured Americans that the conflict with Iraq would be short-lived and cost few American lives. One teacher said,

> I told my social studies class that I thought George Bush paid attention to the critics of the war in Vietnam. Before attacking Iraq, he went to the United Nations, he got a declaration of support from the American Congress, he made sure he got the backing of NATO [North Atlantic Treaty Organization], and he used only volunteers in the combat force. Perhaps . . . our government learned its lesson from what went wrong in Vietnam.[2]

But despite President Bush's reassurances, thousands of antiwar demonstrators poured into the streets of cities and towns across the United States. After the tragedy of Vietnam, these protesters feared that intervention in the Persian Gulf War might signal the beginning of America's involvement in another long, costly war.

The Future

Even after America's success in winning the Gulf War, many people remained concerned that the United States

Despite the success of the American efforts in the Persian Gulf War, there were still fears that the war with Iraq would become another drawn-out conflict like Vietnam. Here, American General Norman Schwarzkopf (left) meets with Iraqi generals to discuss cease-fire terms toward the end of the Persian Gulf War.

might become involved in conflicts in distant parts of the world. Author Tom Wells wrote: "The Vietnam syndrome continues to give Washington pause. But whether it will prevent other unnecessary conflicts is, sadly, open to doubt. . . ."[3]

Author David Boaz wrote:

> In just a few short years since the Persian Gulf War, we have sent American troops, or been urged to send troops, to Somalia, Haiti, Bosnia, Liberia, Rwanda, Burundi, Macedonia, and a host of other places. These places have just one thing in common: no vital American interest is at risk there. Less than a generation after the disaster in Vietnam, we seem to have forgotten the lessons of our intervention there. That intervention, too, started small, with good intentions; no one expected that we would end up with 500,000 American troops there and 55,000 American deaths.[4]

Legacy of the Antiwar Movement

The antiwar movement helped end the Vietnam War, leaving Americans with what seems to be a permanent aversion to participation in foreign hostilities. The movement also spurred the development of increased political activism. Environmental, civil rights, feminist, and animal rights organizations have all reaped the benefits of the experiences of antiwar protesters during the Vietnam era.

Today, the antiwar movement of the Vietnam period is often viewed with nostalgia. In recent years, revivals of 1960s- and 1970s-style clothing, music, and Woodstock-inspired music festivals have found a new popularity, especially among young people who have no personal experience of the Vietnam era. But the legacy of the antiwar movement is more than a style of clothing and music. Its importance lies in the proof that ordinary people can make a difference and can dramatically affect the policies of their government.

★ TIMELINE ★

1954—The Geneva Accords divide Vietnam into two nations at the 17th parallel.

1955—Ngo Dinh Diem becomes the first president of South Vietnam.

1956—Diem requests that France withdraw its troops, and they promise to comply; The North Vietnamese government calls for a military struggle with South Vietnam, causing both sides to build up their military power.

1959—Two American military advisors are killed when Communists attack a military base in South Vietnam.

1961—Vice President Lyndon B. Johnson travels to South Vietnam and promises that the United States will increase aid to the nation; Two presidential advisors recommend that American combat troops be sent to Vietnam to aid in the war against the Communists.

1962—The United States sets up the Military Assistance Command Vietnam (MACV) in Saigon; By June, nearly twelve thousand American military personnel are transported to Vietnam.

1963—In November, Diem and his brother are killed in a coup; President John F. Kennedy is assassinated; Vice President Johnson takes office and announces that he will continue to aid South Vietnam.

1965—Vietcong attack a military base at Pleiku; President Johnson orders the United States military to bomb North Vietnam; President Johnson asks for $700 million in additional aid for South Vietnam; Teach-ins against the war are held on college campuses across the nation.

1967—Large antiwar demonstrations are held in Washington, D.C., and San Francisco; Fifty young men burn their draft cards in Boston.

1968—In the Tet offensive, Vietnamese Communist troops attack major cities in South Vietnam and invade the American Embassy in Saigon; United States troops kill more than one hundred Vietnamese civilians in the My Lai massacre.

1969—President Richard M. Nixon attends peace talks; He announces that the United States will start to withdraw American troops; A Gallup Poll reveals that 58 percent of Americans believe United States involvement in the war is a mistake.

1970—President Nixon announces bombing raids against Cambodia; Protests are held in several major cities and approximately two hundred college campuses are closed; Four students are killed by the National Guard during an antiwar protest at Kent State University, Ohio.

1971—*The New York Times* publishes excerpts from the Pentagon Papers; On April 30, approximately two thousand Vietnam veterans come to Washington to protest the war.

1972—President Nixon orders more bombing raids and the mining of North Vietnamese harbors; Antiwar demonstrators across the nation hold protests against this action; Henry Kissinger and a negotiator for the North Vietnamese government attempt to have peace talks, but the bombing raids resume when negotiations break down.

1973—President Nixon announces that an agreement for "peace with honor" has been reached; Henry Kissinger signs the Paris Peace Accords; American involvement in the Vietnam War ends.

1975—North Vietnamese troops take over Saigon; The Vietnam War is over.

1977—President Jimmy Carter grants a pardon to all Vietnam War draft evaders.

1982—*November*: The Vietnam Veterans Memorial in Washington, D.C., is dedicated.

★ CHAPTER NOTES ★

Chapter 1. The Kent State Shootings

1. Richard Goldstein, *Mine Eyes Have Seen* (New York: Touchstone, 1997), p. 352.

2. Kent State University, "Eyewitness Account of Suzanne Madigan Irvin," *May 4th Exhibit*, n.d., <http://www.library.kent.edu/exhibits/4may95/101irvin.html> (June 17, 1999).

3. Goldstein, p. 352.

4. Ibid., p. 350.

5. "Eyewitness Account of Suzanne Madigan Irvin," <http://library.kent.edu/exhibits/4may95/101irvin.html>.

Chapter 2. The Vietnam War

1. Stanley Karnow, *Vietnam: A History*, 2nd rev. ed. (New York: Penguin Books, 1997), p. 119.

2. Ibid., p. 124.

3. Albert Marrin, *America and Vietnam: The Elephant and the Tiger* (New York: Penguin Books, 1992), p. 39.

4. Loren Baritz, *Backfire: A History of How American Culture Led Us into Vietnam and Made Us Fight the Way We Did* (New York: William Morrow and Co., Inc., 1985), p. 80.

5. Ibid., p. 76.

6. Ibid.

7. Ibid., p. 86.

8. George C. Herring, *America's Longest War*, 3rd ed. (New York: McGraw-Hill, 1996), p. 59.

9. R. Lindholm, ed., *Vietnam: The First Five Years* (East Lansing: Michigan State University Press, 1959), p. 346.

10. Marrin, p. 75.

11. Kim Willenson, *The Bad War: An Oral History of the Vietnam War* (New York: New American Library, 1987), p. 52.

12. Gary B. Nash et al., *The American People, Vol. 2: Creating a Nation & a Society: Since 1865* (New York: HarperCollins College Publishers, 1994), p. 969.

13. Ann E. Weiss, *We Will Be Heard: Dissent in the United States* (New York: Julian Messner, 1972), pp. 66, 68.

14. Marrin, p. 181.

15. E. B. Fincher, *The Vietnam War* (New York: Franklin Watts, 1980), p. 38.

16. Nash, p. 990.

17. Edward S. Herman and Noam Chomsky, *Manufacturing Consent: The Political Economy of the Mass Media* (New York: Pantheon Books, 1988), p. 181.

18. William Dudley, ed., *The Vietnam War: Opposing Viewpoints* (San Diego, Calif.: Greenhaven Press, 1998), p. 247.

19. Don Oberdorfer, *Tet!* (Garden City, N.Y.: Doubleday & Co., 1971), p. 158.

20. Baritz, p. 181.

21. Oberdorfer, p. 195.

22. Robert S. McNamara, *In Retrospect: The Tragedy and Lessons of Vietnam* (New York: Random House, 1995), pp. 266, 269.

23. Weiss, pp. 68–69.

Chapter 3. The Antiwar Movement

1. Melvin Small, *Covering Dissent: The Media and the Anti-Vietnam War Movement* (New Brunswick, N.J.: Rutgers University Press, 1994), p. 2.

2. *WGBH Educational Foundation*, 1997, <http://www.pbs.org/wgbh/pages.amex/1968/68antiwar.html>, (June 17, 1999).

3. William Dudley and David Bender, eds., *The Vietnam War: Opposing Viewpoints* (San Diego, Calif.: Greenhaven Press, 1990), pp. 188, 189.

4. James W. Tollefson, *The Strength Not to Fight: An Oral History of Conscientious Objectors of the Vietnam War* (Boston: Little, Brown and Company, 1993), p. 131.

5. Ibid., p. 6.

6. A. D. Horne, *The Wounded Generation: America After Vietnam* (Englewood Cliffs, N.J.: Prentice-Hall, 1981), p. 25.

7. Kenneth Fred Emerick, *War Resisters Canada: The World of the American Military-Political Refugees* (Knox, Pa.: Knox, Pennsylvania Free Press, 1972), p. 90.

8. Horne, p. 13.

9. Howard Zinn, *The Zinn Reader* (New York: Seven Stories Press, 1997), p. 610.

10. Stanley Karnow, *Vietnam: A History*, 2nd. rev. ed. (New York: Penguin Books, 1997), p. 34.

11. Horne, p. 9.

12. Albert Marrin, *America and Vietnam: The Elephant and the Tiger* (New York: Penguin Books, 1992), pp. 122–123.

Chapter 4. The Vietnam War in the Media

1. Edward S. Herman and Noam Chomsky, *Manufacturing Consent: The Political Economy of the Mass Media* (New York: Pantheon Books, 1988), p. 199.

2. Dorothy and Thomas Hoobler, *Vietnam: Why We Fought* (New York: Alfred A. Knopf, 1990), p. 122.

3. Paul Johnson, *A History of the American People* (New York: HarperCollins, 1997), pp. 886–887.

4. Howard Zinn, *The Zinn Reader* (New York: Seven Stories Press, 1997), p. 609.

5. Herman and Chomsky, p. 178.

6. Jerry Rubin, *Do It! Scenarios of the Revolution* (New York: Balentine, 1970), p. 106.

7. Allan H. Weiner and Anita Louise McCormick, *Access to the Airwaves: My Fight for Free Radio* (Port Townsend, Wash.: Loompanics Unlimited, 1997), pp. 73, 74.

8. Terry Anderson, *The Movement and the Sixties: Protest in America from Greensboro to Wounded Knee* (New York: Oxford University Press, 1995), p. 245.

9. John Orman, *The Politics of Rock Music* (Chicago: Nelson-Hall, Inc., 1984), p. 86.

10. Jon Wiener, *Come Together: John Lennon in His Time* (New York: Random House, 1984), p. 218.

Chapter 5. The Nation Takes Sides

1. Quoted in William Dudley, ed., *The 1960s: Opposing Viewpoints* (San Diego, Calif.: Greenhaven Press, 1997), pp. 104, 105.

2. Barry Goldwater, *The Conscience of a Majority* (New York: Prentice-Hall, Inc., 1970), p. 205.

3. Arlene Schulman, *Muhammad Ali: Champion* (Minneapolis, Minn.: Lerner Publications Company, 1996), p. 62.

4. Ibid.

5. Ibid., p. 63.

6. Ibid., p. 68.

7. Melvin Small, *Covering Dissent: The Media and the Anti-Vietnam War Movement* (New Brunswick, N.J.: Rutgers University Press, 1994), p. 66.

8. Jim Bishop, *The Days of Martin Luther King, Jr.* (New York: G. P. Putnam's Sons, 1971), p. 402.

9. Ibid., p. 448.

10. Ibid., p. 449.

11. Jon Wiener, *Come Together: John Lennon in His Time* (Chicago: University of Chicago Press, 1991), p. 89.

12. John Orman, *The Politics of Rock Music* (Chicago: Nelson-Hall, Inc., 1984), p. 107.

13. Dudley, p. 110.

14. Tom Wells, *The War Within: America's Battle Over Vietnam* (Berkeley: University of California Press, 1994), pp. 579–580.

Chapter 6. The Government Cracks Down on Protesters

1. James Kirkpatrick Davis, *Assault on the Left: The FBI and the Sixties Antiwar Movement* (Westport, Conn.: Praeger Publishers, 1997), p. 8.

2. Ibid., p. 54.

3. Ibid., p. 55.

4. "Group to Publicize FBI's Informers," *The New York Times*, March 26, 1971, p. 27.

5. Davis, p. 16.

6. Lawrence S. Wittner, *Rebels Against War: The American Peace Movement, 1933–1983* (Philadelphia: Temple University Press, 1984), p. 287.

7. Albert Marrin, *America and Vietnam: The Elephant and the Tiger* (New York: Penguin Books, 1992), p. 198.

Chapter 7. Years of Turmoil, 1968–1970

1. Diane Ravitch, ed., *The American Reader* (New York: HarperCollins Publishers, 1990), pp. 344, 346.

2. Ann E. Weiss, *We Will Be Heard: Dissent in the United States* (New York: Julian Messner, 1972), p. 76.

3. Terry H. Anderson, *The Movement and the Sixties: Protest in America from Greensboro to Wounded Knee* (New York: Oxford University Press, 1995), p. 207.

4. Norman Mailer, *The Time of Our Time* (New York: Random House, 1998), p. 681.

5. James W. Tollefson, *The Strength Not to Fight: An Oral History of Conscientious Objectors of the Vietnam War* (Boston: Little, Brown and Company, 1993), pp. 34–35.

6. Loren Baritz, *Backfire: A History of How American Culture Led Us into Vietnam and Made Us Fight the Way We Did* (New York: William Morrow and Co., Inc., 1985), p. 314.

7. Ibid., p. 315.

8. Tom Wells, *The War Within: America's Battle Over Vietnam* (Berkeley: University of California Press, 1994), p. 421.

9. Ibid., p. 427.

10. Anderson, p. 417.

11. William Dudley, ed., *The 1960s: Opposing Viewpoints* (San Diego, Calif.: Greenhaven Press, 1997), p. 39.

12. Ann E. Weiss, *We Will Be Heard: Dissent in the United States* (New York: Julian Messner, 1972), p. 89.

Chapter 8. The Vietnam War Draws to a Close

1. Tom Wells, *The War Within: America's Battle Over Vietnam* (Berkeley: University of California Press, 1994), p. 365.

2. Howard Zinn, *The Zinn Reader* (New York: Seven Stories Press, 1997), p. 393.

3. Dorothy and Thomas Hoobler, *Vietnam: Why We Fought* (New York: Alfred A. Knopf, 1990), pp. 163–164.

4. James A. Warren, *Portrait of a Tragedy* (New York: Lothrop, Lee & Shepard Books, 1990), pp. 171–172.

5. Loren Baritz, *Backfire: A History of How American Culture Led Us into Vietnam and Made Us Fight the Way We Did* (New York: William Morrow and Co., Inc., 1985), p. 344.

6. E. B. Fincher, *The Vietnam War* (New York: Franklin Watts, 1980), p. 73.

7. Baritz, p. 325.

8. Fincher, p. 76.

9. Ibid.

10. Stanley Karnow, *Vietnam: A History*, 2nd rev. ed. (New York: Penguin Books, 1997), pp. 9–10.

Chapter 9. Legacy of the Antiwar Movement

1. A. D. Horne, *The Wounded Generation: America After Vietnam* (Englewood Cliffs, N.J.: Prentice-Hall, 1981), p. 192.

2. James W. Tollefson, *The Strength Not to Fight: An Oral History of Conscientious Objectors of the Vietnam War* (Boston: Little, Brown and Company, 1993), p. 217.

3. Tom Wells, *The War Within: America's Battle Over Vietnam* (Berkeley: University of California Press, 1994), p. 582.

4. David Boaz, *Libertarianism: A Primer* (New York: The Free Press, 1997), p. 253.

★ FURTHER READING ★

Books

Anderson, Terry. *The Movement and the Sixties: Protest in America from Greensboro to Wounded Knee*. New York: Oxford University Press, 1995.

Dudley, William, and David Bender, eds. *The Vietnam War: Opposing Viewpoints*. San Diego, Calif.: Greenhaven Press, Inc., 1998.

Garfinkle, Adam. *Telltale Hearts: The Origins and Impact of the Vietnam Antiwar Movement*. New York: St. Martin's Press, 1995.

Schulman, Arlene. *Muhammad Ali: Champion*. Minneapolis, Minn.: Lerner Publications Company, 1996.

Small, Melvin. *Covering Dissent: The Media and the Anti-Vietnam War Movement*. New Brunswick, N.J.: Rutgers University Press, 1994.

Tollefson, James A. *The Strength Not to Fight: An Oral History of Conscientious Objectors of the Vietnam War*. Boston: Little, Brown and Company, 1993.

Warren, James A. *Portrait of a Tragedy: America and the Vietnam War*. New York: Lothrop, Lee and Shepard Books, 1990.

Wells, Tom. *The War Within: America's Battle Over Vietnam*. Berkeley: University of California Press, 1994.

Wittner, Lawrence S. *Rebels Against War: The American Peace Movement, 1933–1983*. Philadelphia: Temple University Press, 1984.

Wright, David. *Causes and Consequences of the Vietnam War*. Austin, Tex.: Raintree Steck-Vaughn, 1996.

Internet Addresses

Emi's Online Antiwar Anthology. n.d. <http://ftp.std.com/ obi/Emi.Anthology/intro.html> (June 17, 1999).

Kent State University. *May 4th Exhibit*. June 19, 1998. <http://www.library.kent.edu/exhibits/4may95/> (June 17, 1999).

Public Broadcasting Service. "Chicago 1968." *The American Experience*. 1997. <http://www.pbs.org/ wgbh/pages/amex/1968/68antiwar.html> (June 17, 1999).

WWW Virtual Library. *Socialist Republic of Vietnam— History*. n.d. <http://coombs.anu.edu.au/ WWWVLPages/VietPages/WWWVL-Vietnam.html>. (July 3, 1999).

★ INDEX ★